Mentoring disaffected young people

Also available

Sharing a laugh?: a qualitative study of mentoring interventions with young people
Kate Philip, Carole King and Jane Shucksmith

Mentoring disaffected young people

An evaluation of Mentoring Plus

Michael Shiner, Tara Young, Tim Newburn and Sylvie Groben

An SRB multi-agency partnership programme lead by Crime Concern Trust

The **Joseph Rowntree Foundation** has supported this project as part of its programme of research and innovative development projects, which it hopes will be of value to policy makers, practitioners and service users. The facts presented and views expressed in this report are, however, those of the authors and not necessarily those of the Foundation.

Joseph Rowntree Foundation
The Homestead
40 Water End
York YO30 6WP
Website: www.jrf.org.uk

Michael Shiner is currently Senior Research Fellow in the Mannheim Centre for Criminology, LSE. Tara Young is Research Officer at London Guildhall University. Tim Newburn is Professor of Criminology and Social Policy at LSE, and Sylvie Groben is a researcher at the National Centre for Social Research.

This research project began at Goldsmith's College and completed at the London School of Economics.

First published 2004 by the Joseph Rowntree Foundation

ISBN 1 85935 163 8   (paperback)
ISBN 1 85935 164 6   (pdf: available at www.jrf.org.uk)

A CIP catalogue record for this report is available from the British Library.

Cover design by Adkins Design

Prepared and printed by:
York Publishing Services Ltd
64 Hallfield Road
Layerthorpe
York YO31 7ZQ
Tel: 01904 430033; Fax: 01904 430868; Website: www.yps-publishing.co.uk

Further copies of this report, or any other JRF publication, can be obtained either from the JRF website (www.jrf.org.uk/bookshop/) or from our distributor, York Publishing Services Ltd, at the above address.

Contents

Acknowledgements

This was a large and complex study, which depended on the co-operation and support of a great many people. Firstly, and most importantly, we would like to thank all the young people who gave up their time to complete our questionnaires and to talk to us about their lives. We are also very grateful to the mentors who talked to us about their hopes and fears and to the project workers and referral agents who spoke to us about the programme. We owe many thanks to the already overworked and under-resourced project workers who stretched themselves that bit further to ensure that the questionnaires were completed and that the young people were available to talk to us.

The study was funded by the Joseph Rowntree Foundation and Breaking Barriers, and was supported by an Advisory Group chaired by Charlie Lloyd. We are very grateful to our funders for supporting the research and for showing faith in what was a difficult study. We are especially grateful to Charlie Lloyd for his characteristically insightful guidance. Thanks also to Breaking Barriers and Mentoring Plus/Crime Concern for their ongoing support – particularly Claire Reindorp, Lucy Matthews, Amanda Howells and Jan Smith; and to the other members of the Advisory Group – Alan Clarke, Jane Hury, Helen Powell and Mike Stein.

1 Researching mentoring

There is a vast literature, across a range of disciplines, concerned with the 'problems' of youth. Though many of the concerns are long-standing, it is now widely accepted that the transition towards independent adulthood is more uncertain than it once was. As transitions towards employment have been extended so, too, has the period of youthful semi-dependence on adults. While many manage successfully to navigate this increasingly complicated course, a large number experience significant difficulties along the way. There is considerable concern that, either as a consequence of these difficulties, or for other reasons, many young people are deciding against, or being prevented from, participating fully in civil society. It is these young people – who encounter significant problems in the worlds of education, training and employment, are often in trouble with the criminal justice system, or exhibit other forms of problematic behaviour – who are often referred to as 'disaffected'. Responding to, and seeking to prevent or mitigate such difficulties, has become a major focus for public policy. Under New Labour, one of the most talked about (and talked up) forms of intervention with disaffected youth has been 'mentoring'.

Mentoring generally involves establishing relationships between two people with the aim of providing role models who will offer advice and guidance in a way that will empower both parties. Mentoring is believed to hold much promise in reducing youth crime and drug and alcohol misuse, and in increasing social inclusion and attachment to mainstream social values. Indeed, so heavily has it been promoted in recent years that it has become the latest in a long line of 'silver bullets'. Yet, as is so often the case, there has hitherto been remarkably little empirical evidence on which the efficacy of this approach may be assessed. Early mentoring programmes in this area first developed in the United States. 'Big Brothers Big Sisters of America' has become something of a prototype for mentoring schemes and has been influential in the rapid expansion of mentoring on both sides of the Atlantic. Yet, the most thorough review of the research evidence conducted by Sherman and colleagues (1997) for the National Institute of Justice in Washington DC found that community-based mentoring programmes could, at best, be described as only 'promising'. Having reviewed all the evidence, they concluded:

> Even with the encouraging findings from the most recent controlled test of community mentoring, there is too little information for adequate policymaking. The priority is for more research, not more unevaluated programs. The danger of doing harm is far too great to promote and fund mentoring on a broad scale without carefully controlled evaluations.

It is against this background of significant policy interest, rapid development of community-based programmes and an absence of rigorous empirical evidence that this research was designed and conducted. Our focus was on a set of relatively well-established mentoring schemes, each aiming to work with highly disaffected young people.

The study

The evaluation was conducted over a period of a little more than three years (from July 2000 to September 2003), and was based on a combination of quantitative and qualitative methods.

The study focused on a set of programmes, known as Mentoring Plus, and assessed the *process* by which the programme was implemented and the *outcomes* it achieved. The principal objectives were to:

1   examine the process by which vulnerable young people become involved in a mentoring programme and the reasons why other, apparently similar vulnerable young people, decide not to participate

2   consider young people's experiences of participating in a mentoring programme

3   assess the experiences of the staff and those who work as volunteer mentors

4   gauge the impact of mentoring by examining the meanings that mentors and mentees attribute to the processes

5   identify the medium-term impact of mentoring on those young people involved, focusing specifically on:
    •   social engagement (education, training and work)
    •   levels of offending
    •   drug use
    •   general psychological functioning including, for example, self-esteem.

Methodology

The evaluation was built around a longitudinal survey of a large cohort of young people who participated in the Mentoring Plus programme. These young people were to be recruited to the cohort as they joined the programme and completed three questionnaires as part of the evaluation: one as they joined the programme, one as the programme came to an end (the 12-month follow-up) and another six months later (the 18-month follow-up). The surveys were augmented by quantitative information collected directly from the programmes and by a substantial qualitative component – depth interviews were conducted with project staff, mentors, young people and referral agents, and detailed observations were made of the key elements of the programme.

One of the key issues facing the evaluation was how to measure success. Put simply, how could we attribute any changes that were observed in the young people to the programmes? To provide the basis for rigorous assessment, a series of comparisons were built into the design of the study. First, ten programmes were included in the evaluation and this offered an opportunity for partial validation, as it meant that we could compare outcomes for individuals passing through different programmes. Second, we sought to recruit a comparison group from applicants who initially expressed interest but, for differing reasons, decided not to participate in the programme. The comparison group was to be recruited at the same time as the main cohort and we envisaged that the young people in the comparison group would complete the questionnaire on two occasions: once at the beginning of the mentoring programme and again as part of the 12-month follow-up.

Preparation and design

The survey covered a wide range of areas, including demographic characteristics, education, training and work, offending and contact with the criminal justice system, substance use, attitudes and lifestyle. Wherever possible, we included questions from other surveys, partly because they were tried and tested and partly because they provided the basis for comparison with the general population. Much of our questionnaire was derived from the 1998/99 *Youth Lifestyles Survey* (*YLS*) and it also included formal scales to measure self-esteem (Rosenberg, 1965) and locus of control (Robinson et *al.*, 1991). The questionnaire that was developed for the first phase of the survey provided the basis for those that were used in subsequent phases and all of these questionnaires were designed as self-completion questionnaires (that is, they were to be completed directly by the respondents themselves).

In total, 378 young people were recruited to the cohort group and 172 were recruited to the comparison group. In the event, the comparison group was made up of primarily young people who expressed an interest in the Mentoring Plus programme but did not, for whatever reason, go on to participate in it. In a small number of cases, all applicants were included on the programme and project workers recruited members of the comparison group via visits to the schools, youth clubs and Youth

Offending Teams (YOTs) with which they worked (32 young people were recruited to the comparison group in this way). The numbers of young people who participated in the follow-up surveys are shown in Figure 1. The 18-month follow-up concentrated on those members of the cohort who had responded to the 12-month follow-up and successfully included more than half of these young people (54 per cent). However, some young people who had not responded to the 12-month follow-up attended meetings for the 18-month follow-up and were included in the survey.

Across the ten projects, the follow-up rate varied quite markedly according to the degree to which young people had engaged in the programme. Those who engaged most actively in the programme were also the most likely to have been successfully followed up: 71 per cent of those who were highly engaged responded to the first follow-up survey and 54 per cent responded to the second follow-up survey.[1] For all analyses based on the follow-up surveys, data were weighted to reflect the level of programme engagement that was evident in the overall cohort.[2] This was important, as it guarded against overstating the possible impact of Mentoring Plus.

Figure 1 Response to the surveys

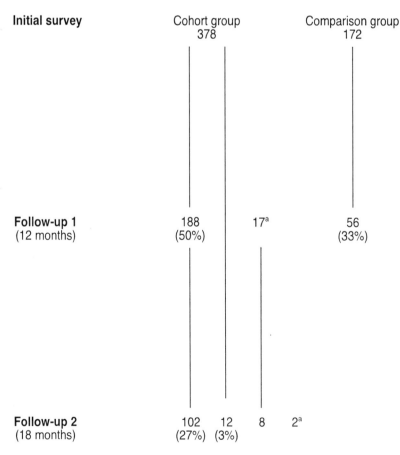

	Cohort group				Comparison group
Initial survey	378				172
Follow-up 1 (12 months)	188 (50%)	17[a]			56 (33%)
Follow-up 2 (18 months)	102 (27%)	12 (3%)	8	2[a]	

a No responses previously received from these individuals.

In addition to the surveys, depth interviews were conducted with over 100 individuals involved in the programmes; including project workers (25), referral agents (20), mentors (40) and young people (36). Observations were also carried out at almost 150 project sessions and events, including recruitment events, programme activities and staff meetings. Interviews and observations were spread across the ten programmes, although there was a degree of concentration in order to allow particular attention to be focused on four case study projects.

Considerable thought was given to the way in which mentors and mentees were selected for the depth interviews. Males and females were well represented in both groups: 14 of the mentors were male and 26 were female; and 22 of the young people were male and 14 were female. And care was taken to ensure that interviewees reflected the overall ethnic and age profile of each group. Twelve 'pairs' of mentors and mentees were interviewed and a series of guidelines were developed to ensure that the sample reflected a range of issues that might be influential in determining the nature of the mentoring relationship. Parings where male mentors were matched with male mentees, where female mentors were matched with female mentees and where female mentors were matched with male mentees[3] were included, and relationships where the partners shared a common ethnic heritage and where they did not were also included. In 12 cases, the young people were interviewed on two separate occasions, as it was felt this would provide the basis for more detailed insights than one-off interviews.

Mentoring Plus

The mentoring projects studied in this research were run by Crime Concern and Breaking Barriers,[4] and were based on the widely acclaimed and award-winning Dalston Youth Project (DYP). Established in 1994 by Crime Concern, DYP was one of the first formal mentoring projects in the UK and is widely considered to have been a successful and pioneering project (Benioff, 1997). DYP targeted disaffected young people and sought to build their basic education, employment skills and confidence through a one-to-one mentoring relationship with an adult volunteer drawn from the local community and a structured education and careers programme. Within two years, DYP had been identified by the Audit Commission as an example of good practice (Audit Commission, 1996) and a period of expansion followed as Crime Concern established a series of new projects, known as Mentoring Plus, based on the DYP model. By 2000, projects had been established in eight London boroughs, Manchester, and Bath and North East Somerset.[5]

These projects aimed to:

- reduce youth crime and other at-risk behaviour

- help at-risk young people back into education, training and employment

- enable community members to get involved in solving community problems through volunteering (Crime Concern, undated[a]).

All ten projects shared a similar structure (see Figure 2; and also Benioff, 1997). Steering committees included representatives from local agencies with an interest in combating disaffection and reducing crime (e.g. Social Services, Education Welfare, Police, Probation, Local Regeneration programmes and Training and Enterprise Councils) and played a key role in monitoring the projects and supporting their development. Each project was linked to Crime Concern by a consultant who was responsible for strategic and thematic-based support, which covered issues such as funding, staff employment, training and support, policy decisions and changes to programme content/structure. The core staff team was typically made up of four distinct posts – Project Manager, Education Co-ordinator, Mentor Co-ordinator and Administrator – although, in practice, the roles of Education Co-ordinator and Mentor Co-ordinator were sometimes combined.[6] In many of the projects, youth workers were employed on a sessional basis to deliver and support components of the education programme.

Seventy-five members of staff were employed across the ten Mentoring Plus projects during the period covered by the study. Mentoring Plus included a particular focus on black and minority ethnic communities, particularly those of black African/Caribbean

Figure 2 Organisational structure of Mentoring Plus

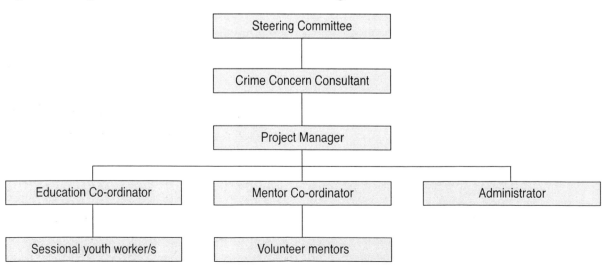

heritage (Crime Concern, undated[b]), and this was reflected in the composition of the staff teams. Slightly more than half (54 per cent) of those employed by the projects were black African/Caribbean; just over a third (37 per cent) were white; less that one in ten (8 per cent) were mixed race and the remaining 1 per cent were Asian.

The projects recruit young people (aged between 15 and 19 years) twice a year onto cycles spaced six months apart, usually in the autumn and then again in the spring. Following the design of DYP, they offer mentoring alongside an education/training component and this 'Plus' element of the programme covers issues such as literacy, numeracy and basic life skills (e.g. job search and interview skills). Each programme runs for ten to 12 months and typically starts with a residential.

- *Residential courses*: residentials last for three days and the aim is to build trust between young people and mentors through a mixture of physical outdoor activities and indoor sessions. Outdoor activities are designed to help establish relationships and co-operation while indoor sessions aim to enable young people to develop positive, achievable goals for the coming year. At the end of the residential, young people are matched with volunteer mentors.

- *One-to-one mentoring*: following the matching, the young people and mentors are expected to meet once a week for the duration of the programme. The aim is to provide positive and supportive role models to young people who have previously experienced very difficult relationships with adults. Mentors are trained to help young people work towards their new personal objectives and they may also act as 'outreach workers' linking individuals with local services that they would otherwise fail to access.

- *An education/training programme*: this part of the programme aims to provide the young people with the complementary practical life skills and educational/training opportunities needed to support their new personal goals. The education component concentrates on improving the young people's interpersonal and presentation skills, literacy and numeracy, and personal motivation and effectiveness. Classes are designed and led both by in-house project staff and in partnership with existing local providers. Young people have the option of receiving accreditation for their work. During the period covered by the evaluation most projects ran at least one education/training session a week although some ran up to three such sessions a week.

Each new cycle starts with a recruitment drive for mentors and young people. Young people are recruited onto the project in several ways, the most common being the referral from statutory and community agencies and, less frequently, through outreach work in local communities and youth clubs or via friends and/or family members. Once referred, each young person is subject to an interview and selection process and, if accepted, attends an induction session where they learn more about Mentoring Plus, mentoring, the education sessions and the commitment required by them. Participation in the project is voluntary. Young people are free to decline to become involved and, similarly, the projects may reject referrals they deem to be inappropriate, although this rarely occurs in practice.[7]

Mentoring Plus has a structured process of recruiting mentors primarily through advertising in local, national and specialist (*The Voice, New Nation, The Big Issue*) newspapers, though the Mentor Co-ordinator responsible for the recruitment is free to employ other methods.

Application forms are distributed to those volunteers who have expressed an interest in becoming a mentor, and the volunteers are invited to attend an introductory session to learn more about the project and to meet current mentors. The introductory session is followed by a police search and an extensive training programme for the volunteers, which culminates in the residential.

Until the residential, or at least until the pre-residential evenings, the young people and volunteers have followed separate pathways into mentoring. The residential presents a pivotal point in the Mentoring Plus experience for both groups (see Figure 3). Henceforth, they will start the process of familiarisation and begin working with each other to facilitate the mentoring component of the programme. Matching young people with a volunteer begins the mentoring process, which continues throughout the year they are involved in the project. In addition to mentoring, the young people are encouraged to take part in other programme activities such as educational workshops, project group nights and social events, which are permeated with support from project staff. Similarly, volunteer mentors are offered support – in the form of one-to-one and group sessions – from the Mentor Co-ordinator, which is then supplemented by additional training.

Towards the end of the cycle, around two months before the end of the mentoring year, the projects co-ordinate an 'ending session' for mentors designed to help them develop strategies for concluding the relationship with their mentee and to discuss any future relationship they may have with them.[8] This session also provides a platform for mentors to discuss any reservations they may have about ending their relationships with the project and to receive guidance on how to terminate it successfully. Subsequently, the project holds a graduation ceremony to recognise the achievements of both mentors and mentees, and to formally end the programme for a particular cycle.

Figure 3 Programme structure

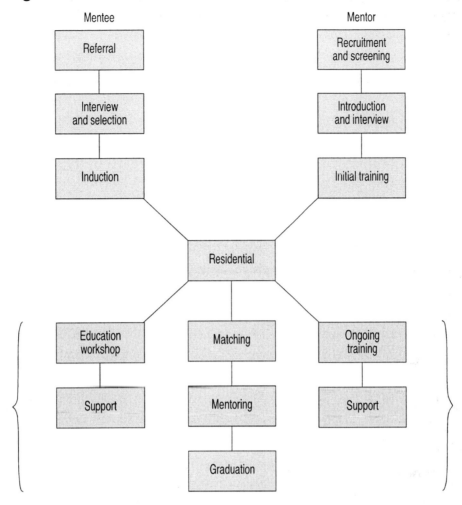

2 Introducing the young people and the mentors

The young people

The demographic characteristics of the young people who were recruited to Mentoring Plus are shown in Table 1. At the time of joining the programme, the vast majority of the young people were 15 to 16 years old. Males outnumbered females by about two to one and most of the young people were from black and minority ethnic groups, although whites made up the largest single group. Most of the black and minority ethnic young people recruited to the programme were from black Caribbean, black African or mixed race backgrounds and very few were from Asian backgrounds. Only one project recruited Asian young people, and even here the proportion recruited was low compared with their demographic representation in the local borough.

The ethnic profile of the young people on the programme clearly reflected the location of the projects, although the low level of Asian involvement could not be explained in this way. Black African/Caribbean communities tend to be concentrated in London (Modood *et al.*, 1997) and were well represented in most of the London-based projects. Predictably, those projects that were based outside of the capital had the lowest level of black and minority ethnic representation. The number of black

Table 1 Demographic characteristics of the young people (per cent in the cohort)

Demographic characteristics	%
Age	
12–14	17
15	45
16	25
17–19	13
	100
Sex	
Male	70
Female	30
	100
Ethnicity[a]	
White	43
Black African/Caribbean	41
Asian	2
Mixed race/dual heritage	14
	100

Source: Mentoring Plus cohort (first survey).

n = 428.

a Please note that the total percentage amounts to 101 per cent, as the figures shown have been rounded to the nearest whole number.

African/Caribbean young people on the programme also reflected the focus on social exclusion and the particular orientation of Crime Concern/Mentoring Plus. Black and minority ethnic groups are particularly vulnerable to processes of exclusion and marginalisation (Crime Concern, undated[b]) because they face a 'double disadvantage', which comes from being concentrated in deprived areas and facing particular forms of racial discrimination (Cabinet Office, 2000). Young people from some groups, particularly those of black Caribbean heritage, are over-represented among school excludees and within the criminal justice system (Bowling and Phillips, 2002). Partly in response to these patterns of disadvantage, Crime Concern (undated[a]) produced a briefing paper for mentoring work with minority ethnic young people, in which it stated, 'we focus particularly on schemes for Black British, African and Caribbean youth from a youth justice perspective, because this is the area in which we have most expertise'.

Routes into Mentoring Plus

The young people followed a variety of routes into Mentoring Plus (see Figure 4). Most were formally referred by other organisations, most commonly Youth Offending Teams (YOTs) and schools. Self-referral was also a relatively important route into the programme. Depth interviews highlighted the important role that 'word of mouth' played for these young people, as many of them heard about the project from friends.

Figure 4 Route into Mentoring Plus (per cent in cohort)

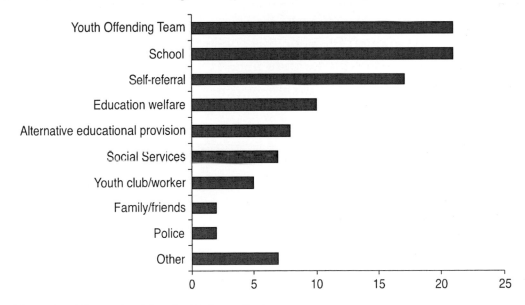

Source: Mentoring Plus cohort (project information).
$n = 349$.

During the depth interviews, many of the young people described Mentoring Plus in ways that invoked the image of a traditional 'youth club'. They saw the project as providing a place to have fun and to 'chill out'. Many of them viewed the residential as a 'holiday' and this constituted a key factor in their decision to join:

> I just come along because it is a weekend away, so I thought that I might as well, but I didn't actually know about you getting yourself a mentor and everything – I just thought that it was an activity weekend kind of thing.
> (Young person)

Alongside this theme, however, it was generally recognised that Mentoring Plus offered more than opportunities for recreation. While some of the young people were attracted by the prospect of the one-to-one confidential relationship, and expected to be 'sitting down and having a chat with someone', many were motivated by the desire to change some aspect of their lives:

> If you come here they can put you on little courses and stuff, things to do instead of getting into trouble. So I started coming … Because I thought like going on the way that I'm going on I'm going to go in prison soon, so I thought I don't want to go down that route, I've got to sort myself out … I just thought that *[Mentoring Plus]* was going to be about like, a place to chill out and people to talk to, people to help out with problems and keep you off the streets.
> (Young person)

A similar pattern was evident from the first survey. On the one hand, a sizeable proportion of the young people indicated that escaping boredom had been a factor in their decision to join Mentoring Plus and this confirmed the importance of general entertainment-based activities (see Figure 5). On the other hand, specific goal-oriented objectives were also an important source of motivation and considerable congruence was evident between the aims of the programme and the young people's reasons for joining: the desire to stop getting into trouble and gaining access to employment and/or training were key motivational factors, while the desire to get back into school/college and to improve relationships were also significant for a sizeable minority of participants.

Figure 5 Reasons for joining Mentoring Plus (per cent in cohort)

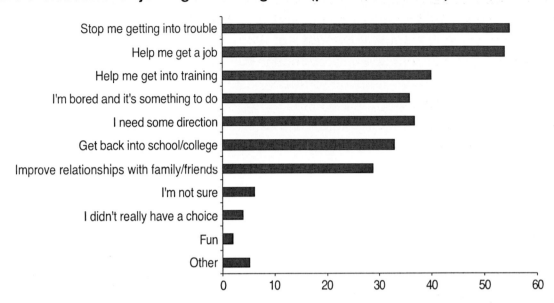

Source: Mentoring Plus cohort (first survey).
n = 371.

Social exclusion and risk

As already noted, Mentoring Plus's key aims were to have some impact on offending and other forms of at-risk behaviour and to help disaffected young people back into education, training and employment. This focus, and indeed this language, reflects the now well-established empirical evidence, which suggests that there are a number of readily identifiable 'risk factors' in childhood and adolescence that heighten the likelihood of problems later in life. These include: parental conflict and separation; early involvement in offending, drinking and drug use; and disruptive behaviour at school. To begin to fulfil its aims, therefore, Mentoring Plus had first to recruit young people who might reasonably be described as 'at risk' in one or more of these ways.

Judgements about the extent to which the young people recruited to the programme were socially excluded or at risk could only really be made in comparison with the general youthful population. The 1998/99 *Youth Lifestyles Survey* (*YLS*) played a key role in this regard, as it facilitated precisely this type of comparison (Stratford and Roth, 1999). Based on a nationally representative sample of nearly 5,000 young people, the *YLS* covered many of the same issues as our evaluation and, as such, provided a robust benchmark.[1]

Family background

The contexts within which the young people were living implied a strong degree of family disruption and breakdown. Comparison with data from the *YLS* confirmed that levels of family disruption within the Mentoring Plus cohort were very high. Less than a fifth (19 per cent) of young people in the cohort were living in traditional nuclear families, that is, with both their natural mother and father and/or brothers and sisters, compared with two-thirds (65 per cent) of similarly aged young people in the general population. More than half of the Mentoring Plus cohort (54 per cent) were living in single-parent households, the vast majority of which (92 per cent) were headed by their mother. And this was more than double the proportion of young people in the general population who were living in single-parent households (19 per cent).

In addition, high levels of dissatisfaction with the quality of family relationships were evident and this was particularly marked in regard to relationships with natural and/or step-parent(s). Non-existent or problematic relationships with (step)fathers were particularly noteworthy. Overall, about one in six young people in the Mentoring Plus cohort indicated that they did 'not get on at all well' with their mother and/or father (17 per cent with their mother and 15 per cent with their father). In addition, 4 per cent of young people appeared not to be in contact with their natural mother. And two in five (40 per cent) indicated that they were not in contact with their natural father.

Education, training and work

There is little doubt that Mentoring Plus successfully targeted young people who were facing, or were likely to face, considerable difficulties in the transition from school to work. And, once again, comparisons with the *YLS* put into sharp focus the particular difficulties facing the young people who joined the programme. These young people were much more likely than those in the general population to be disengaged from education, training and work (40 per cent compared with 4 per cent – see Table 2). More specifically, while they were more likely to be on a training scheme, they were much less likely to be attending school, studying at college or university, or to be working. They were also much more likely to dislike school and to truant on a regular basis and this is reflected in the relatively high proportion who reached the school-leaving age without any GCSEs.[2] The qualifications profile of the young people involved in Mentoring Plus also suggests that many of those who went to college did so, initially at least, to compensate for their lack of GCSEs, hence the relatively large proportion with NVQ Foundation/Intermediate qualifications.

Table 2 Current status, orientation to school and qualifications (per cent)

	Mentoring Plus cohort	General youthful population[a]
Current status[b]		
Attending school	46	74
Studying at college/university	8	13
On a training scheme	5	2
Working	1	7
Disengaged	40	4
Truanting from school[c]		
Every week	34	5
Two or three days a month	18	1
Less often	17	14
Not at all	31	79
Attitudes to school		
Like it a lot	16	35
Like it a little	22	35
Neither/nor	21	14
Dislike it a little	11	7
Dislike it a lot	30	9
Qualifications (17–19 year olds only)		
GCSE	47	82
NVQ Foundation/Intermediate	17	3
BTEC Certificate	2	4
City and Guilds	13	6
No qualifications	45	9

Source: Mentoring Plus cohort (first survey, n = 353) and YLS (1998/99, n = 1,680).

Note: the 1998/99 YLS was adjusted to reflect the age and sex structure of the Mentoring Plus cohort.

a   Confidence intervals were produced for estimates based on the YLS (at the 0.05 level) and are shown in Table A1.1 in Appendix 1. In all but one case, the figure for the Mentoring Plus cohort was outside the confidence interval for the estimate based on the YLS and, in most cases, it was well outside this range.

b   The 46 per cent of the Mentoring Plus cohort who were attending school included those who were attending a special education unit (10 per cent of the total cohort) and those who were truanting regularly (9 per cent of the total cohort). The YLS did not distinguish special education units from schools, nor was it possible on the basis of the YLS to identify young people who were excluded from school or who were truanting regularly. Young people in the Mentoring Plus Cohort who were excluded from school were included in the disengaged category.

c   The figures given here relate to the cohort as a whole and include those who were in school at the time of the survey and those who had already left. Our question about truanting was not strictly comparable with the question used in the YLS. We asked about truanting during the last year or the last year that the young person attended school, while the YLS asked about truanting in relation to 'secondary school'.

Offending and contact with the criminal justice system

The vast majority (93 per cent) of young people involved in Mentoring Plus had committed at least one offence at some point in their lives and most (85 per cent) had done so during the previous 12 months.[3] On average, they had committed six of the offences listed in the survey with four having been committed in the last year. No clear patterns were evident in relation to which types of offence were most widely committed: while some violent offences (such as public disorder) were among the most widely committed, others (such as carrying a weapon to attack someone) were among the least widely committed; similarly, while some property offences (such as stealing something worth £5 or more) were relatively widespread, others (such as snatched something from the person) were relatively unusual.

By grouping these specific offences into broader categories, it became clear that most of the young people in the cohort were generalist rather than specialist offenders.[4] Very similar rates of offending were apparent in relation to violent offences, property offences and criminal damage (see Table 3). Traffic violations were somewhat less common and this reflects the age structure of the young people involved in Mentoring Plus, as many of them were below the age at which they could legally drive. Among those young people who had offended during the previous 12 months, less than a quarter (22 per cent) restricted themselves to offences within a single broad category and well over half (57 per cent) committed offences in three or four of these broader categories.

Data from the *YLS* confirmed that levels of offending within the Mentoring Plus cohort were high (see Table 3). Young people in the cohort were more than twice as likely as those in the general youthful population to have committed an offence during the previous 12 months and were between three and four-and-a-half times as likely to have committed an offence within each of the broad categories during this period. Differences between these populations were even more marked in relation to persistent and serious offending: the young people in Mentoring Plus were nearly six times as likely as those in the general population to be persistent offenders[4] and were seven times as likely to have committed a serious offence[6] during the previous 12 months. In view of this, there can be little doubt that many of the young people involved in Mentoring Plus were among the most prolific of young offenders.

The higher rate of offending within the Mentoring Plus cohort was particularly marked in relation to violence. Young people in the cohort were more than four-and-a-half times as likely as those in the general youthful population to have committed such an offence during the previous 12 months. And it was clear that some of this offending was very serious. One in two (50 per cent) of the young people in the cohort

Table 3 Comparative rates of offending (per cent)

	Mentoring Plus Cohort	General youthful population[a]
Committed an offence		
No, never	7	42
Yes – but not in last 12 months	8	20
Yes – in last 12 months	85	38
	100	*100*
Criminal damage		
No, never	31	67
Yes – but not in last 12 months	16	18
Yes – in last 12 months	54	15
	100	*100*
Property offences		
No, never	27	71
Yes – but not in last 12 months	14	13
Yes – in last 12 months	60	16
	100	*100*
Violent offences		
No, never	22	76
Yes – but not in last 12 months	14	10
Yes – in last 12 months	64	14
	100	*100*
Traffic violations		
No, never	50	78
Yes – but not in last 12 months	8	10
Yes – in last 12 months	42	13
	100	*100*
Persistent offender[b]		
No	38	89
Yes	62	11
	100	*100*
Serious offence		
No, never	30	85
Yes – but not in last 12 months	13	7
Yes – in last 12 months	57	8
	100	*100*

Source: Mentoring Plus cohort (first survey, n = 376) and YLS (1998/99, n = 1,254).

Note: the 1998/99 YLS was adjusted to reflect the age and sex structure of the Mentoring Plus cohort.

a For the confidence intervals, please refer to Table A1.2 in Appendix 1.

b The Mentoring Plus survey did not include questions about the frequency with which offences were committed and this measure of persistence is based on the range of offences committed: those young people who had committed three or more of the specific offences we asked about during the previous 12 months were classified as persistent offenders. Recent research has shown that the volume of young people's offending is very strongly correlated with the breadth of their offending so that those who commit the broadest range of offences tend also to commit the greatest number of offences (Smith and McVie, 2003).

indicated that, during the last 12 months, they had carried a weapon to defend themselves, one in five (19 per cent) indicated that they had carried a weapon to attack somebody and one in four (26 per cent) indicated that they had hurt somebody with a weapon. While it has been established that there is a close relationship between offending and victimisation (Smith and McVie, 2003), this distinction may be particularly blurred in relation to violent offences. It is, for example, worth noting that more than twice as many young people in the cohort carried a weapon for the purposes of defence rather than attack. During conversations and interviews, many of the young people highlighted ways in which they routinely managed the potential for violence that grew out of 'street culture', gang rivalries and territorialism. For many, this involved carrying a knife and, for some, it meant carrying a gun. In some cases, the consequences were fatal or near fatal. During the course of the fieldwork, we became aware that two young people associated with the programme had been stabbed to death and that two of the young people on the programme were seriously injured as a result of knife attacks.

Given their level of offending, it is, perhaps, unsurprising that most of the young people in the cohort had received some kind of sanction from the criminal justice system. Nearly two in three (62 per cent) had been cautioned by the police, nearly one in two (47 per cent) had been arrested and charged with an offence, more than one in four (26 per cent) had been convicted of an offence in court and one in eight (12 per cent) had spent time in a Young Offenders' Institution or in Local Authority Secure Accommodation. Moreover, the bulk of these young people's contact with the criminal justice system was relatively recent (i.e. mostly within the last 12 months). As a point of comparison, the 1998/99 *YLS* indicated that approximately one in 20 (5 per cent) of young people in the general population had been cautioned during the previous 12 months, one in 50 had been taken to court during this time and one in 200 (0.5 per cent) had ever spent time in a Young Offenders' Institution or in Local Authority Secure Accommodation.[7]

Drinking and smoking

The vast majority of young people involved in Mentoring Plus had drunk alcohol and smoked cigarettes at some point in their lives, and many continued to do so. At the time of joining the programme, almost half (48 per cent) were smoking every day and a third (33 per cent) were drinking at least once a month. Many of these young people appeared to be drinking infrequently, although most had been drunk in the previous 12 months: one in ten (10 per cent) had been drunk at least once a week during this period, a further one in six (17 per cent) had been drunk at least once a month and a further two in five (40 per cent) had been drunk less often than this, leaving one in three (33 per cent) who had never been drunk. While rates of smoking in the Mentoring Plus cohort were very high compared with the general youthful population, rates of drinking were *relatively* modest. The proportion of daily smokers in the cohort was approximately three times that in the general population (48 per cent compared with 12–17 per cent). By contrast, while almost two-thirds of the young people in the cohort drank less than once a month, this compared with less than half those in the general population (61 per cent compared with 37–44 per cent). And only one in five drank on a weekly basis compared with approximately one in three of those in the general youthful population (21 per cent compared with 30–37 per cent). The rates of drunkenness that were evident within the cohort also appeared to be unremarkable.[8] To some extent, the relatively moderate rates of drinking that were evident in the Mentoring Plus cohort reflected its ethnic composition. There is some evidence that young people from black and minority ethnic groups drink less than white young people (for an overview see Newburn and Shiner, 2001)[9] and this pattern was evident in the Mentoring Plus cohort.

Illicit drug use

Most of the young people in the Mentoring Plus cohort had used an illicit drug at some point in their lives and most had done so within the last 12 months (72 per cent and 62 per cent respectively). As in the general population, cannabis was by far the most widely used illicit drug and more than half (60 per cent) of the young people in the cohort had used this drug during the previous 12 months. Almost all the young people in the cohort who had ever used an illicit substance had used cannabis and many restricted themselves to this drug: two in three users (69 per cent) had only ever used cannabis and this accounted for half (49 per cent) the total cohort.[10] As well as being the most widely used illicit drug, cannabis was also the most intensely used: almost three-quarters (72 per cent) of current cannabis users and more than a third (38 per cent) of the overall cohort were using this drug on a weekly basis, and it is likely that around half of these young people were doing so every day.[11]

Approximately one in five (22 per cent) of the young people in the cohort were poly drug users, that is they had used more than one illicit substance. Some way behind cannabis, cocaine was the second most widely used illicit drug followed by ecstasy, amphetamines and solvents (see Table 4). These substances were not widely used, however, and their regular use was limited to a very small minority. Two per cent of the cohort had used cocaine at least once a week during the previous 12 months and a further 1 per cent had done so at least once a month. Similar rates of use were evident in relation to the hallucinants[12] (2 per cent had used one of the substances in this category at least once a month and the same proportion had done so at least once a week). Any use of heroin and, to a lesser extent, crack cocaine was very unusual and only 1 per cent of the cohort had used *either* of these substances on a weekly or monthly basis. This is particularly noteworthy given the centrality of these substances to the drugs–crime nexus, which dominates current policy.

Table 4 Comparative rates of illicit drug use (per cent)

	Mentoring Plus cohort	General youthful population
Cannabis		
Used in the last 12 months	60	24
Used but not in last 12 months	10	6
Never used	30	70
	100	*100*
Hallucinants		
Used in the last 12 months	10	9
Used but not in last 12 months	5	5
Never used	85	86
	100	*100*
Solvents		
Used in the last 12 months	4	4
Used but not in last 12 months	3	4
Never used	93	92
	100	*100*
Cocaine		
Used in the last 12 months	7	1
Used but not in last 12 months	3	1
Never used	90	98
	100	*100*
Crack and/or heroin[a]		
Used in the last 12 months	4	0.3
Used but not in last 12 months	3	0.5
Never used	94	99
	100	*100*

Source: Mentoring Plus cohort (first survey, n = 345) and YLS (1998/99, n = 1,630).
Note: the 1998/99 YLS was adjusted to reflect the age and sex structure of the Mentoring Plus cohort. Percentages do not always add to 100 due to rounding.

a   These substances have been combined because of the small number using them and because they provide the basis for what is typically thought of as being 'problematic' use. Recent analysis has also shown that use of these substances tends to go together (Parker and Bottomley, 1996; Shiner, 2003).

Patterns of illicit drug use in the cohort differed from those in the general youthful population in a number of important ways (see Table 4). Surprisingly, perhaps, it was not simply the case that levels of use were higher among young people involved in Mentoring Plus as their *relative* rates of use varied between substances. While hallucinants and solvents were used at very similar rates in the two populations, striking differences were evident in relation to cannabis, cocaine and crack/heroin. Young people in Mentoring Plus were two-and-a-half times as likely as those in the general population to have used cannabis during the previous 12 months and were more than five times as likely to have done so on a weekly basis (38 per cent compared with 7 per cent). They were also seven times as likely to have used cocaine[13] in the previous 12 months and 13 times as likely to have used crack or heroin (5 per cent of the cohort had used crack at some point in their lives and 2 per cent had used heroin).

Social exclusion?

The young people recruited onto the Mentoring Plus programme had experienced multiple forms of disadvantage and were at considerable risk of becoming isolated from mainstream social, economic and cultural life. Many of them had experienced substantial disruption in their schooling and family lives. Truancy and disengagement were widespread and many of those who had left school had done so without any qualifications. In addition, levels of offending, illicit drug use and contact with the criminal justice system were much higher than in the general youthful population. They were, to use currently popular terminology, a group for whom social exclusion was a very real prospect.

Case study: Solomon's[14] story

We first interviewed Solomon when he was 17 years old. Describing himself as a 'thug', he talked of his involvement in local gang life and how he had been to court for a series of violent incidents, including stabbings and shootings. Solomon felt he had been surrounded by trouble since he was young. During his childhood, the police had regularly come to the house looking for his cousins and older brother who was sent to prison when Solomon was 13 years old. He said: 'My cousins raised me and I picked up their thug mentality'.

Solomon initially went to the same secondary school as his older brother and felt that his family's reputation had made school life difficult for him. He felt his teachers expected him to behave like his brother and that the other pupils were scared of him. His education was disrupted when he was moved to another school, which he described as being 'thugged out' and 'a big ghetto'.

Solomon had mixed feelings about his family life. He said 'I haven't really got a family, there is only my brothers and sister and my mum and it has always been broken; we have never been one'. His mother had tried to protect him when he was little and, although he did not get on well with her, he said he would always be grateful to her. It upset him to see her struggle on her own. When we interviewed Solomon for a second time, almost a year later, he said he was still unable to talk to his mother: 'because when I sit with my mum it is like I can feel her pain and I know when she is upset, and I would rather avoid it than see it, so I just can't be around my mum'.

By this time, Solomon was at college and had come out of the gang scene, although, he said, his former involvement still had repercussions. He said: 'I'd

(Continued overleaf)

21

got myself into situations with big men and it has actually put me in my place because I thought I was bad but I got myself in situations and it could get very serious'. Solomon had seen people he knew go to prison and had suffered from sleeplessness and anxiety after being shot at. He felt that the birth of his niece had been a 'turning point' and he described feeling responsible for her and 'calm' when he was with her. Solomon was thinking about his future and was particularly looking forward to having a family of his own.

Mentors

The socio-demographic profile of the mentors differed markedly from that of the young people involved in the programme. Although most of the mentors (like most of the mentees) were from black and minority ethnic groups, the majority of the mentors (in contrast to the young people) were female (see Table 5). Taken as a whole, the mentors also formed a much more socially included group than the young people. Predictably, perhaps, given what is known about volunteering, over three-quarters (78 per cent) of mentors were in full- or part-time employment, 11 per cent were students and 10 per cent were unemployed. Of those in work, over half (54 per cent) held senior, professional or associate professional posts;[15] nearly one-fifth were administrators or secretaries (18 per cent); one in eight (12 per cent) worked in the personal service industry; and very few were skilled or elementary workers (5 per cent). Just over one-tenth (13 per cent) reported having been convicted of a criminal offence, mainly for relatively minor offences such as shoplifting or traffic violations.

The mentors on the programme revealed a variety of motives for their involvement, which could be divided broadly into those that were 'instrumental' and those that were 'normative' (see box below; and, for discussion, Sherroff, 1983). Although the distinction between these different types of motivation is analytically useful, it is important to recognise that they are not mutually exclusive and are often intertwined. Instrumental motivations are those that derive from a deliberate strategy; in other words volunteering is a means to an end of some kind, such as employment. Normative or moral motivations are those that encompass the desire to do something, the right thing, or what is good and proper.

Table 5 Profile of mentors (per cent)

	%
Sex	
Males	31
Females	69
	100
Age	
18–24	13
25–34	47
35–44	29
45–54	9
55–64	2
	100
Ethnicity	
White	44
Black African/Caribbean	47
Asian	4
Mixed race	4
Other	1
	100

Source: Mentoring Plus (project information).
n = 453.

Mentors' motivations for volunteering

Instrumental

1 Work experience and career progression
  • To enhance job prospects.
  • To gain experience of working with young people.

2 Substitute for work
  • Unsatisfied in current job.
  • Frustrated at work.
  • Wanted reprieve from work.
  • Wanted to work in area that made a difference.

3 Personal development or family circumstances
  • To be involved in an activity that would make them a better person.
  • To gain insights into young people that would help them to raise their own children.
  • To compensate for their own negative experiences of family life as young people.
  • To do something rewarding, challenging and more personal.
  • To do something else in life besides going out and having fun.

(Continued overleaf)

4 Enhancement of social life
- To fill spare time.
- To meet others, as spend most of time alone.

Normative/moral

1 Societal concern or contribution
- To get to know culture and society in local area.
- To do something or give something back to the community.
- To have impact on crime in local community.

2 Concern for young people
- To learn about young people and lifestyle.
- To help and understand young people.
- To help delinquent young people.
- To work with young people from black and minority ethnic groups, especially young black men.
- To compensate for not being able to foster a young person.

3 Sense of duty
- To help people less fortunate.
- To provide people with a listening ear.
- To make a contribution to the disadvantaged.
- Had a mentor when they were young and wanted to continue tradition.

One of the main motivating factors for becoming a volunteer mentor was the opportunity that Mentoring Plus provided for individuals to learn new skills, and acquire qualifications and experience related to working with young people:

> I might want to pursue a career in working with young people, I thought that it would have been a good way to start … that's why I chose this.
> (Mentor)

Mentoring also provided people with a starting point from which they could develop and enhance their career potential without having to give up the security of their current position:

> I was always working with adults and I wanted a taste of working with teenagers. But I didn't want to leave my job just in case I hated it. So I thought if I could do it on a voluntary basis I can be working with teenagers, working with offenders, ex-offenders and that way I could do both. Kill two birds with one stone and still get paid.
> (Mentor)

The desire to develop an understanding of teenagers prompted some individuals to become involved in Mentoring Plus. Losing touch with young people, their lifestyle and what it meant to be young was a concern for these mentors who believed that mentoring could better their understanding of young people and the obstacles they faced. Some wanted to challenge prejudicial attitudes and preconceptions they had about young people:

> I just had to take a look at myself and I thought I could hear myself moaning, do what most people do, they always moan about young people on the bus on the way home from work ... and I felt myself falling into that trap and I stopped and thought, what are you doing? You swore that you was never gonna be like this! You were young once and that was how you acted!
> (Mentor)

The majority of volunteers talked about their concern for young people and the impact this had on their decision to become mentors. They felt that some young people, depending on cultural, racial, physical, sex and class differences, were unable to deal with the challenges faced as they moved into and through puberty. Overall, the volunteers saw this as a stage in the lives of young people that was difficult to negotiate and they wanted to help smooth their passage through this turbulent time by listening to, or empowering them. This was particularly the case for those people who wanted to help young black men.

> I wanted to go to the heart, so to speak, into the heart of trying to do something positive and it said about role models, role model. I often hear negative things about black men. I'm a black man and if they say black men then that doesn't exclude me that puts me right in it. So that was the real reason the depth of why I went into mentoring and why I felt I had something to offer.
> (Mentor)

Becoming a mentor

Prior to becoming involved in Mentoring Plus, the majority of volunteers had no previous experience of working with young people in a formal setting and few had worked with disaffected young people. Of those interviewed, ten had been mentored (informally) in the past or had mentored someone else (four of whom had previous experience of mentoring at Mentoring Plus). One volunteer had mentored for another mentoring organisation. Despite their lack of formal voluntary experience, they felt they possessed enough personal experience to benefit the young people they would be working with. As prospective mentors, these volunteers were subject to several weeks of training, which began with an introductory evening and ended with the residential.

According to Benioff (1997), Mentoring Plus training should last four days (spread over two weekends), be administered by an external training team and include the following components:

*   background information on the project, the young people and the local area

*   discussion, role-play, word-storming, etc. on issues facing disadvantaged young people

*   discussion of peer pressure, racism, sexism, homophobia

*   development of listening skills and non-judgemental counselling skills

*   information on local agencies providing services for young people

*   dos and don'ts of being a mentor

*   what to expect on the residential and other components of the project.

In practice, some variation from this format was evident in most projects. Although some projects ran blocks of training over two weekends, others provided training over six evenings or half days. While training at four of the ten projects was initially led by an external provider and was accredited by local colleges, there was, during the course of the evaluation, a move towards in-house training: by the end of the study, only one project was using an external provider. The content of training also varied between the projects, although most managed to include the majority of the topics outlined above.

Three-quarters of the volunteers interviewed said the training provided at Mentoring Plus had prepared them for mentoring. They described the training as 'good', 'intensive' and 'thoroughly enjoyable'. And felt it had helped them to challenge their own stereotypes of young people, to listen and not to judge, to become more tolerant and respectful of young people while, at the same time, remaining firm.

> *[The training taught me]* the frame of mind of some of the young people and the frame of mind you actually had to be in to do this work effectively and actually to be of use to these people and just to make you address issues that you might not have addressed yourself.
> (Mentor)

[The training taught me] how to react and respond in different situations … and things that you thought were … with training and discussion with other people, I realised that … if I handled it in another manner then I could avoid negative reactions and have positive … more positive feedback.
(Mentor)

Once the in-house classroom training was completed, the mentors were invited to attend a three-day residential. The residentials were held at an activity centre outside the local vicinity and involved the mentors and young people in challenging indoor and outdoor activities designed to build self-awareness, respect, co-operation, trust and partnership (Benioff, 1997). It presented an opportunity for the mentors to get to know the young people, to see how well they work with each individual in the group and to practise the skills learnt during the training period. As the residential represents the first major meeting between mentors and young people, it is often the part of the training process that causes most anxiety for the mentors. Essentially, the residential is about mixing with the young people, which for some mentors is something they have not done in a long time:

The training was good but actually going on the residential I felt was, I suppose, far more useful in the training of myself as mentor. Actually being able to be with young people is something that I've not really done for a long, long time.
(Mentor)

It is a place where the mentors come face to face with disadvantaged young people and have to confront their views, feelings and preconceptions about them. This made some mentors feel exposed and vulnerable, especially if they did not feel comfortable in the role of mentor or felt they had nothing in common with the young people:

[I felt] scared and nervous. You know like kept questioning myself, you know. Is this what you really want? Are you sure you know what you are doing? I suppose it's being accepted as well by the young people, you know. You've not met them before the residential … It's like 60 people that you've sort of like have to try and bond with and so it can be quite scary, but I'm glad I did it!
(Mentor)

Being exposed to young people in this personal way helped, as one mentor said, to promote communication, patience, tolerance, understanding and, ultimately, acceptance. For a large proportion of mentors, the residential provided a foundation on which to formulate working relationships with the young people and gave them something to talk about when they met them again.

A central theme that emerged from the interviews was one of personal development. The mentors felt that they had acquired new skills and ways of working with young people. Through the experience of mentoring, the volunteers were confronted with the world of disadvantaged young people, some of whom had difficult and complex lives. As a result of this experience, some of the mentors felt they had become more patient and non-judgemental or more responsible, confident, organised and tolerant. The mentors with children believed that mentoring had helped them to relate more fully to their own children and provide better parenting. Two mentors, one male one female, went on to pursue a career in youth work. Above all, mentoring dispelled some of the anxieties the mentors had about being around and working with young people; they felt able to understand and relate to them 'on a deeper level'.

Conclusions

1   Mentoring Plus successfully identified and recruited a group of disadvantaged and disaffected young people who were involved in high levels of offending and were at considerable risk of social exclusion.

2   Mentoring Plus successfully targeted young people from some black and minority ethnic communities.

3   The young people recruited to Mentoring Plus identified specific reasons for joining the programme, which were consistent with its aims and objectives.

4   Mentoring Plus successfully recruited a diverse range of mentors to work with the young people, including a large proportion from black and minority ethnic communities (mainly black African/Caribbean).

5   In general, the socially excluded nature of the young people involved in the programme contrasted markedly with the profile of the mentors. Most of the mentors were currently employed, many of them in professional or associate professional posts. A small proportion, however, were either unemployed or had a criminal conviction.

3 Mentoring in practice

As we outlined earlier, the mentoring programmes that were at the heart of this study had two main components. They sought to establish a one-to-one relationship between the young people and an adult assigned to them – their 'mentor'. Alongside this relationship, the programmes also provided a significant educational/training element – the 'Plus' bit of Mentoring Plus. In this chapter, we examine both of these elements of the programme, from the initial residential that the majority of young people attended, through to the end of the young person's relationship with the programme (at some point during the course of the year).

We begin by looking at the issue of programme integrity. Previous research on many forms of social intervention has highlighted the central importance of implementation in understanding how interventions work (and whether they have any impact). In particular, an unfortunately large body of research has shown how failed implementation often lies at the heart of the apparent absence of success in interventions. Understanding project integrity is important therefore in helping us make sense of young people's engagement with the projects, as well as providing crucial contextual information for our discussion of impact in the next chapter.

Programme integrity

Programme integrity has recently been identified as a key influence on the development of successful interventions. This notion covers a range of distinct, but related, issues including programme design, management and staffing. For a programme to have a high level of integrity it must employ skilled practitioners, the stated aims should be linked to the methods being used and management should be sound (Hollin, 1995; McGuire, 1995). In essence, programme integrity is less concerned with programme content than with the process by which it is implemented, delivered and managed. According to Hollin (1995, p. 196), it 'simply means that the programme is conducted in practice as intended in theory and design'.

The integrity of the Mentoring Plus programme varied markedly across the ten projects included in the evaluation. Although none of the projects implemented the programme exactly as it is outlined in the literature (there was, for example, very little evidence of college 'taster' courses), we concluded that four of them had achieved a relatively high degree of programme integrity: staff turnover in these projects was low and/or well managed and the main elements of the programme were implemented as planned.[1] Three of the projects achieved a moderate degree of integrity (staff turnover was reasonably well managed and some of the key elements were implemented as planned) and three achieved a low degree of integrity (staff turnover reached problematic levels and elements of the programme were consistently delayed or did not occur at all).

Four factors stood out as key influences on the integrity of the programme.

1 *Staffing*: while the majority of staff said they enjoyed working at Mentoring Plus, they also commonly reported being 'overloaded', having to work unreasonably long hours and having to 'cram stuff in to each day'. These pressures translated into a high degree of 'burn out', as nearly half (49 per cent) of the staff involved in the projects had left Mentoring Plus by the end of the evaluation. In some projects, staff shortages meant that elements of the programme had to be postponed or cancelled and downward spirals were established in which staff turnover and implementation failure fed off one another to create a sense of crisis: staff shortages meant that elements of the programme were postponed or cancelled, which undermined staff morale and, potentially, led to further departures. Although Mentoring Plus staff were, on the whole, well qualified and highly experienced for their roles, once projects were caught in a downward spiral, they often appointed new members of staff who had little by way of relevant qualifications and experience:

> I think just recently with the recent cycle, it's probably been the most difficult cycle yet and … having one member of staff on long-term sick leave and having the manager away for a couple of weeks during the quite critical point of recruitment and not having an administrator at that time which meant there was just one full-time member of staff and three part-time sessional staff … I kind of made the decisions I thought were right for the project … and give ourselves a deadline, if we don't get the young people in and we don't get the mentors by that date then we're not going to do it.
> (Project worker)

2 *Longevity*: newly established projects were particularly vulnerable to high staff turnover, to downward spirals and to low levels of programme integrity. Six projects were established in the year before the evaluation started and, of these, four experienced a high degree of staff turnover and three achieved a low level of programme integrity. Three projects that were established at the same time or one year earlier achieved a high degree of integrity and none of them experienced anything more than a low level of staff turnover. Only one project achieved a high degree of programme integrity in the face of moderate or high staff turnover and this reflected a robustness that it had developed over time: it is no coincidence that this project had been running the longest out of all those included in the evaluation.

3   *Location*: the location of the projects formed a recurring theme in interviews with project workers. Only one of the projects occupied premises on its own and this was considered important by the workers: 'the young people are free to roam about here and that's been fundamental to the success of the project'. The remaining projects shared premises with other community groups and workers voiced concerns that the projects were inaccessible and/or unappealing because they were located a long way from where the young people lived and/or because they were based in unsafe and inappropriate locations:

> I mean, I think the venue can be a problem, where we are, I think the venue … I've heard from young people that it's not safe around here at night and stuff like that really and it's an issue for the walking home and this sort of gang culture, and territorial, you know, you're in my area … that kind of issue as far as engagement goes.
> (Project worker)

One of the projects ceased to operate temporarily as it relocated from premises in an area which the workers considered to be unsafe. Another project had to postpone elements of the programme, as its premises were flooded and another project had to vacate its premises when they were declared unsafe by Health and Safety inspectors.

4   *Funding*: financial difficulties were identified as an important threat to programme integrity. Some of the project workers felt the programme would have been better implemented and would have a greater impact if funds had been available to provide additional specialist services. In more extreme cases, it was suggested that elements of the programme could not be implemented because of insufficient funding and, on occasion, short-term difficulties had long-term consequences. One of the project managers felt that the project had never recovered from an initial shortfall in funding and, while the more recently established projects were most vulnerable to funding 'crises', the longer-term projects were not immune from them: financial difficulties were heavily implicated in the closure of three of the projects before the end of the evaluation.

These influences combined to create what were often unstable and unpredictable environments in which to work. Considerable disruption was evident across the projects; many experienced high levels of staff turnover and some simply ceased to operate. By the end of the evaluation period, four out of the ten projects had closed down, one faced an uncertain future, as it had ceased to operate and two had withdrawn from the Mentoring Plus umbrella. Some such disruption is common, if not endemic, within the voluntary sector, particularly in circumstances where future funding is far from guaranteed and organisations are caught up in a merry-go-round of fund-raising. Although far from unique, this operating environment is of central importance in understanding the nature of the Mentoring Plus projects, for it affects every aspect of their operation and shapes the experiences of project staff, mentors and young people.

Engaging with young people

While programme integrity provides a useful framework for considering the impact of mentoring, there are some more immediate questions that must be addressed first. We have already seen that Mentoring Plus successfully identified a highly disadvantaged, often disruptive, socially detached group of young people. The next question to consider is: to what extent did it engage them?

Approximately two in three (69 per cent) of the young people referred to Mentoring Plus were recruited on to the programme. Information about their levels of engagement was provided by the projects and was classified according to the following criteria.[2]

- *Not engaged*: did not attend the project and was not given a mentor.

- *Minimally engaged*: attended the project and/or met their mentor every couple of months or less often.

- *Moderately engaged*: attended the project or met their mentor at least once a month.

- *Highly engaged*: attended the project and met their mentor at least once a month.

The vast majority of young people recruited by Mentoring Plus engaged with the programme on some level. Less than one in six did not engage at all, while the rest were divided fairly equally between the different levels of engagement (see Figure 6). Broadly similar levels of engagement were evident in relation to the project and the mentors (46 per cent of the young people engaged actively with the project and 40 per cent engaged actively with the mentors).[3]

Figure 6 Levels of engagement with Mentoring Plus (per cent in the cohort)

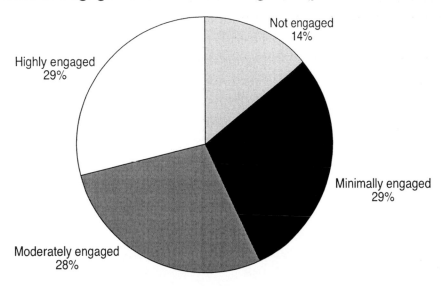

Source: Mentoring Plus cohort (project information).
n = 391.

Overall rates of engagement with Mentoring Plus varied according to the young people's demographic characteristics, although differences between groups tended to be fairly modest. Young women tended to engage more actively than young men (46 per cent engaged actively compared with 37 per cent) and young people from black and minority ethnic groups tended to engage more actively than white young people (46 per cent of black Africans/Caribbeans and 43 per cent of mixed race young people engaged actively compared with 35 per cent of whites).[4] Going against the general trend, however, a very low rate of engagement was evident among South Asian young people (only 10 per cent of those who took part in the recruitment process engaged actively with the programme).[5] Very little variation was evident according to age.

Rates of engagement also varied according to the key dimensions of current activity and levels of offending. Crucially, Mentoring Plus appeared fairly effective in engaging those young people who were at most risk of social exclusion. In terms of current activity, the young people who were studying at college/university, or who were on a training scheme or were in paid work were the least likely to engage actively with the Mentoring Plus programme (29 per cent), suggesting that they may have felt the focus on social exclusion was less relevant to their circumstances. While the highest rate of engagement was evident among those young people who were attending school or a special education unit (43 per cent engaged actively), similar rates of engagement were evident among those who were truanting regularly or were completely disengaged from education, training and work (38 per cent and 39 per cent respectively). In addition, those young people who offended persistently during the previous year were just as likely to engage actively as those who committed fewer offences (38 per cent of each group). Those who committed serious offences, however, were less likely to engage actively than those who had not done so (35 per cent compared with 47 per cent). Notable differences were also evident according to family structure, with the young people who had experienced greatest disruption being the most likely to engage actively (51 per cent of those living in care, with foster parents or in a hostel; 44 per cent of those in reconstituted families; 42 per cent of those in single-parent families; 31 per cent of those in the 'other' category; and 26 per cent of those living in nuclear families).

In seeking to explain these levels of engagement, a number of factors may be considered important. The projects did not assume that the young people would simply attend the programme and invested a considerable amount of time and energy building relationships, encouraging them to attend the programme and supporting them in various aspects of their lives: this involved frequent telephone calls, text messages, letters, passing messages on through friends, home visits, talking through problems and, in some cases, attending police stations and court. In addition, a range of incentives were built into the fabric of the programme. These included money, vouchers, food and social activities/entertainment that would appeal to the young people (such as bowling and laser-quest). Within the London projects, moreover, the notion of 'cultural competence' may have been a key factor (Sangster *et al.*, 2002). It seems likely that specific attempts to address the needs of black African/Caribbean youth, which included the recruitment of large numbers of black African/Caribbean staff and volunteers, contributed to the successful engagement of young people from these communities.

The mentoring relationship

At the end of the residential, mentors and young people were asked to nominate three people that they would like to work with and matches were announced at a 'matching meeting' one or two weeks later. Although the projects sought to match people who had chosen one another, it was not always possible and some mentors and young people were matched with people they had not nominated. Matches were not made in any precise or scientific way and indeed the process varied across the projects. In general, young people were matched with people they 'got on with' or with mentors with particular personal characteristics, skills or experiences that were deemed to be appropriate and relevant: in one case, for example, a young person who wanted to work in the music industry was matched with a mentor who had strong connections in that area. Personal characteristics were also taken into account so, for example, male mentors were not matched with female mentees. Although the projects did not follow a policy of strict ethnic matching, there was a tendency to match mentors and mentees with a shared ethnic heritage.

After the matching meeting, the mentors and the young people with whom they had been matched were expected to identify the key issues on which they would focus and this provided the basis for an 'action plan'. Ideally, the action plan should be developed by both partners and in most cases the areas identified reflected the programme's main aims and objectives: reducing offending and other anti-social behaviour, or getting back into education, training or employment.

Numerous attempts have been made to understand and model mentoring relationships. By and large, such models are linear in construction, following the relationship from its inception through different stages to its eventual conclusion. These models oversimplify the nature of mentoring and tend to overstate the centrality of goal-focused, instrumental activities. By idealising mentoring in this way, such models assume that young people will move relatively quickly into activities that either challenge some aspect of their behaviour or remedy some deficit in their social functioning (such as literacy and numeracy difficulties or other education- or work-related issues). Though such models may have some didactic value, they do not reflect the complexity and diversity of mentoring relationships and tend to underplay the relatively mundane nature of much mentoring activity. Consequently, they may lead to unrealistic expectations among participants, funders and policy makers. We offer an alternative way of looking at mentoring that is both more nuanced and realistic. In this model, we describe the 'ordinariness' of much mentoring activity and offer a conceptual framework that highlights the cyclical and reactive nature of many mentoring relationships. We go on to consider how such relationships are managed by those involved before, finally, identifying a range of qualities that characterise 'successful' relationships.

Towards a model of mentoring

While mentoring relationships are often presented in linear form, our research suggests that in practice they are typically *cyclical* in nature. In its most basic form, for example, the mentoring relationship involves contact being made, a meeting being arranged and then undertaken. The activities involved when the parties meet are generally fairly mundane – having tea/coffee, playing pool, shopping, bowling, or perhaps going to the cinema. Almost all mentoring relationships will begin this way. Most will continue in this fashion for some time before they can progress further. Often, in fact, relationships do not progress much beyond this, if at all. This cycle of 'contact-meeting-doing' we refer to as the 'basic cycle'.

Difficulties with the idealised action-oriented approach were evident very early on in most relationships, as, in practice, constructing an action plan proved problematic. Many young people were unable to identify things that they wanted to change, while others simply did not turn up to the meeting. This is not to say that there were no examples of formal action planning between mentor and mentee at the outset of the relationship. And, where such planning did occur, moreover, it tended to move the relationship beyond the 'basic cycle':

> Right from the beginning he wanted help finding a job. He wanted help with learning about skills for jobs. He wanted someone just to go round with him because at first he didn't have any confidence to go and ask if they had any vacancies. I used to go round with him. He used to pour out all of his problems and all of the things he has been through.
> (Mentor)

Such action-oriented behaviour so early in the relationship was rare, however, and, contrary to the picture often held of mentoring, much of what happened had little obvious connection with responding to challenging behaviour or the causes or consequences of social exclusion. It was the mundane, humdrum stuff of basic human interaction that provided the staple diet for most mentoring relationships. This should not lead one to underestimate their importance, however, as it is precisely the repetition of such activities that helps to build familiarity and, with luck, eventually trust. And, as studies of other quasi-therapeutic relationships have found (Newburn, 1993; Mair et al., 1994), it is often vital that some form of practical engagement is established before any more substantial form of intervention can be attempted (if it is at all):

> I have told her stuff from a couple of times after meeting her and nothing has come back to me whatsoever, so then I brung it on a little bit more and nothing's come back to me and I brang it on more and more and then, in the end, I just let out everything and then nothing came back to me, do you know what I mean. And so, if she did go and say something like, to one of her mates, it wouldn't bother me, but if she told someone who like lives locally and then the word goes round that's when I would be really pissed.
> (Young person)

Given this, it is unsurprising, perhaps, that engaging in challenging, action-oriented activity in the context of mentoring relationships proved difficult. Moreover, while most relationships did not move beyond the 'basic cycle', this should not necessarily be considered problematic. And, arguably, only becomes so if there are expectations – on the part of the mentor, mentee or the project – that successful mentoring relationships will necessarily go beyond this stage.

Where relationships did progress, they often did so in response to a problem or crisis (e.g. homelessness, family breakdown, specific forms of offending, substance misuse, violent behaviour). As already noted, proactive planning and action was relatively rare, particularly in the early stages of a relationship, and it was more often the case that problems emerged during the course of meeting that the mentor needed to deal with. As such, mentoring relationships may be considered to be *reactive*. Because movement beyond the 'basic cycle' often involved reacting to a difficulty or problem that arose, we refer to this element in the relationship as 'firefighting'. Again, the relationship tended to be experienced cyclically with the emergence of an identifiable pattern where, in response to some problem or crisis, the contact-meeting-doing cycle extended into a 'contact-meeting-doing-firefighting'. This firefighting element of the relationship came as a surprise to many of the mentors, especially those who held to the more ideal-typical model and, while some of them engaged actively with the issues that arose during this period, others were less able to cope and experienced difficulties around boundaries and emotions:

> I initially thought it would maybe mean meeting once a week for a couple of hours but the young person that I was matched with, it's been like, some weeks it's been like contact seven days a week, you know if she's had a real difficult problem that she's had to deal with and it has meant, yeah, I've had to give her more support and I've had to go out and meet her. Sometimes I don't think the other volunteers understand that the contact is maybe a little bit more than what they actually think.
>
> (Mentor, see Cheryl's story later in this chapter)

Having progressed to the firefighting stage, it is, as with the basic cycle, possible for a mentoring relationship to remain there for a considerable period. Once a particular problem had been dealt with, however, many relationships returned to the basic contact-meeting-doing cycle. That is to say there is no necessary progression to a more advanced stage. Relationships may stay in the firefighting cycle, revert to the basic cycle or, in some cases, progress beyond the reactive firefighting stage, to become genuinely action-oriented and closer to what often appears to be the ideal-typical conception of mentoring.

More usually, where relationships did move into an action-oriented phase, this occurred fairly late on, once trust had developed and issues were identified. Then, more creative activities (with, say, time being spent engaged in job hunting or in internet cafes perfecting and sending CVs) could be identified and undertaken:

[At first] she didn't really talk about family and stuff, and then it was only after that we sort of started, she started talking to me in little bits and bobs … I suppose, definitely, she has learned to trust me, you know that must have been a big, really big thing for her … In the first few months I didn't want to push it about her getting a career and this that and the other, because basically she wasn't ready, you could just tell straight away, she was here there and everywhere in her head, you know. I just wanted to befriend her really, I just wanted her to sort of just be able to come up and say, 'can we go out for a chat?'. The first half of the year was definitely just more like going out every week and chatting, her getting to know as much about me as possible because I thought that would be quite important and then I'd slowly try to bring a little bit of structure and we did our action plans.
(Mentor)

Once again, this process was experienced and may be presented, as a cycle of activity. The 'action-oriented cycle' tended to be either a four- or five-stage process depending on whether firefighting was necessary (contact-meeting-doing-[firefighting]-action). As a means of simplifying and understanding the mentoring relationship, we may therefore identify three potential cycles:

- the basic cycle: contact-meeting-doing

- the problem-solving cycle: contact-meeting-doing-firefighting

- the action-oriented cycle: contact-meeting-doing-[firefighting]-action.

In Figure 7, these cycles appear from left to right along an arrow indicating the start and end of the mentoring relationship. Though linear in appearance, this should not be taken to imply that we see there being any necessary progression from one cycle to another. Although possible, such progression is not inevitable. Mentoring relationships may never proceed beyond the basic cycle or, alternately, having reached either the problem-solving or action-oriented cycle, may then revert to the basic cycle. As the surrounding box indicates, the basic cycle is in many ways the staple of the mentoring relationship, and, even in those cases where the relationship has 'moved on' to problem solving or to action, it may revert at any time to the basic cycle. As with relationships more generally, there is no clear and simple path that can be charted in mentoring. Indeed, this is even more the case given the fragile nature of most mentoring relationships.

Figure 7 A model of the mentoring relationship

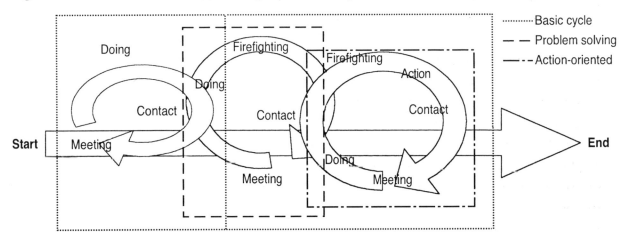

Starting and managing the relationship

At almost any stage, the relationship between mentor and mentee may break down. Failure to keep appointments is frequently cited as a reason for breakdown (though it may also be a consequence of course) and there are many other potential sources of dlfference and even conflict. For both mentor and mentee, the relationship is one that requires considerable investment and trust, and is one that is experienced – perhaps particularly when it does not move beyond the basic cycle – as a rather fragile entity. This fragility is generally ever present in the mentoring relationship, though it is especially visible in the early stages.

> Well, I tried to make contact with him quite a few times and he didn't make contact back with me. And that is the truth. I lost motivation because I didn't want to feel as though I was stalking him and putting him under pressure to meet up. I did put quite a lot of effort into it.
> (Mentor)

> I don't know, I never felt that I could really talk to her. It was just kind of a still atmosphere when I was with her. So I didn't really like it that much.
> (Young person)

In the early stages, the projects are proactive in arranging interaction between the mentor and the young person. Structured activities are organised by the project with the aim of establishing basic contact and to introduce and begin a process of demystifying the idea of mentoring. The start of the mentoring relationship, however, signals the point at which the mentors take greater charge of the relationship and what happens within it. Not many of the young people commented on their first meeting with their mentor (outside of the residential setting). Those who had not been allocated the mentor of their choice or who had not attended the residential (selection by proxy) reported having had a positive experience/impression of their mentor at their initial meeting, where they saw him/her as showing an interest in how they felt, as understanding, and where their mentor appeared to be fun to be with:

> She rang me up and said we would meet in McDonald's and that she would be wearing a red coat. I went there and I see someone in a red coat. I went to her and I said 'hello, is your name Jenny?', and she said 'yeah' and from that day we just started talking, we went in the restaurant and had something to eat, we chatted for about two hours. She was a really nice woman, she was all right to talk to as well, she was understanding, that is why I got along with her I reckon.
> (Young person)

Generally, the young person and their mentor would arrange where to meet and what to do by mutual agreement, either from one session to the next or over the telephone, depending on the schedules of both mentor and mentee. Perhaps not surprisingly given the somewhat chaotic lives that many of the young people led, turning up for meetings was by no means guaranteed. Simply 'not being bothered' was one of the main reasons that young people gave for failing to keep appointments or, linked with this, they felt they had other more important, or more attractive options:

> I disliked the time I had to take. Sometimes I couldn't be bothered to meet her, sometimes I could be, but back then I was a little kid and I wanted to go out and play football. *[But]* my mum would find out; she would slap me on my head and say 'go' and I would just go.
> (Young person)

In addition, in response to the survey, approximately one-quarter (27 per cent) of the young people said that they did not feel that they needed a mentor and one-third (31 per cent) said that they could not really relate to their mentor. Under such circumstances, establishing a relationship between mentor and young person was especially problematic. These are tricky human relationships, which have considerable potential for rupture – and by no means just because of the behaviour of the mentee:

> I was supposed to go to the job centre that day or something, but told her *[the mentor]* that I was feeling a bit ill. 'Oh any excuse' *[she said]*, and I was telling her the truth … I told her to get off my fucking line and I switched off the phone.
> (Young person)

However, even when contact was made and the basis of a relationship established, the failure to keep appointments was one of the key 'stress points', often causing the relationship to break down. The impact of such breakdown on the young person depended in part on their attitude to mentoring, and also on their relationship with the mentoring project more broadly. Where they felt supported by the project, they sometimes felt that the mentor was less important. In practice, the majority of the young people developed quite strong and positive relationships with one or more of the project workers, and at times would see 'the people in the project [as] more like my mentors than my actual mentor'. Only a small minority (8 per cent) of the young people mentioned that they did not get on with the workers at Mentoring Plus. Where they had a less supportive relationship with the project, however, feelings that their mentor was not 'sticking with them' could be particularly upsetting.

> My boyfriend went in jail and I did phone her a bit late, I think it was about half 11. But I needed that support but even if she didn't pick up the phone she would have had a missed call and it would have said from Sara. And she didn't phone me back and I thought … that was a bit out of order because she could have phoned me to see if I was all right. She must have known that something was wrong with me because I don't normally phone her that late … I thought that I could rely on her because she told me that I could rely on her … I have told her that I have lost weight, I lost a stone, that is how depressed I am, so the thing that she could do is at least phone me.
> (Young person)

Speaking to Sara five months later, she had not been in contact with her mentor since. On the whole, in relationships where project workers and/or mentors were clear about boundaries, and where the young people felt supported by the project, a telephone call not received or a meeting having to be rearranged was less problematic than it might be in other circumstances; the longer the relationship was established the less likely it was to break down:

> There are occasions when [the mentor] has not turned up but there are occasions she has had a really good excuse not to turn up. But having said that it doesn't really bother me because … even when you first meet you're asked to understand that they have got to work and they have got their own life as well as being there for you, they've got their own lives and they have got their own things to sort out, so they can't be there with you 24/7 but they can be there the majority of the time. Sometimes, she doesn't phone me, but I don't think anything of it, that she has got her own life and that she will phone me when she is ready.
> (Young person)

41

Qualities of successful relationships

A number of characteristics of a 'successful' mentor, or mentoring relationship, were identified by the young people, of which five appeared to be key:

1 *Being able to talk* :

   I could tell her anything, and there was a lot of things that I couldn't speak to other people including my friend and I spoke to *[my mentor]* about it and it helped me, because I got it all off my chest, you know speaking about it.
   (Young person)

2 *Reciprocity* :

   I gave her the basics before I could get a bit deep – I have trouble at home with my mum and at school and this, that and the other, and she was like 'OK then'. And we spoke and stuff and then later … she told me stuff about her. Saying it made it easier for me to talk as well, because, I was like, 'OK then, she is not like a robot or anything like that'. So yeah it was all right. And then, just the other day I saw her and she was upset because her friend did commit suicide and she was the last one that he saw, so I was like 'OK then', and I was talking to her and that, not brought her out of her shell, but I was talking to her until she felt relaxed and that she could talk. And she said to me 'thank you'.
   (Young person)

3 *A relationship based on respect rather than authority* :

   In our school structure, teachers are supposed to be higher than you, therefore you've got to respect them and they don't have to respect you, but with a mentor you have to respect them and they have to respect you, so it's completely different.
   (Young person)

4 *Understanding, and being interested in, young people* :

   [Mentors are] genuinely interested in what is going on in your life, and they are not just there because it is a job, because as far as I'm aware they are like volunteers so they are not getting paid, so they can't really pretend because there is nothing in it for them.
   (Young person)

5   *Having fun* :

> *[Mentoring]* is about people helping you, like giving you advice when you need
> it, someone to talk to, someone to confide in, someone to have a laugh with,
> someone to go out with and things like that.
> (Young person)

Only a minority of young people saw their mentor all the way through until the official
end of the mentoring relationship, one year later. In addition to the premature
breakdowns of relationships, described above, in some cases, the relationship would
come to a natural end during the course of the year because the young person felt
that they did not really need their mentor any more, or had moved on or either the
young person and/or mentor was too busy and involved in too many activities to
keep up the relationship. The majority of those who saw their mentor for the full year
said that they were hoping to keep, or were still keeping, in contact. For some, this
meant that they would still meet their mentor, albeit less frequently. Those who were
still seeing each other mentioned that at this stage the nature of the relationship had
changed:

> Our season is kind of over soon ... But we still carried on meeting each other
> over Christmas time, even like Mentoring Plus didn't have nothing going on.
> Now it is not even like mentor and mentee, it is just like big friend, little friend,
> that is what it is like after a while. I think that is the whole point of it like, you can
> go past a certain stage, so you can drop the barrier, so yeah.
> (Young person)

Case study: Cheryl's story

Cheryl was in her mid-to-late 20s when she volunteered to become a mentor,
after seeing an advert in a local newspaper. She had children of her own and
had considerable experience of working with young people but wanted to work
with young adults and felt that being a mentor would help her to become a youth
worker. At the residential, Cheryl spent quite a lot of time with Dawn and the two
of them were subsequently matched with one another:

> One of the things we particularly laugh about is that we were both
> frightened of heights and we were on this assault course, and I remember
> thinking to myself, there's no way I'm going there, forget that, and she was
> really terrified, and I was encouraging this young person, 'yeah, go on climb
> that tree, you'll be pretty safe up there'.
> *(Continued overleaf)*

Dawn was living in residential care and, although Cheryl was nervous about being a mentor, she felt well prepared: 'I've come to the project with my eyes open anyway, cause I'd worked with teenagers in care, and I'd dealt with teenagers that don't want to bond and don't want to speak to you'. Cheryl had also left home at a young age and felt she could relate to Dawn and understand her. After an initial 'testing' period, Dawn began to 'open up' and told Cheryl how frightened she was of being alone:

> It took a bit of time for the young person to trust me, you know she was very inquisitive about why I was on the project, 'why do you want to do this when you're not getting paid?', you know, sort of them questions at first ... At the beginning I think she was cautious as to what she was telling ... we could have a laugh and joke about the residential and that was OK but when it comes to talking about problems that she had and things needed sorting she would tell me part of the story but she wouldn't tell me the whole story. And then maybe a couple of days later she'd phone and say, 'oh, I didn't tell you this the other day' ... But over a period of time, the relationship has changed ... and it's just now totally different and more trusting.

Over the course of the year, Dawn went through some 'bad times'. She suffered a bereavement and was moved from one care home to another. During these times, Cheryl spoke to Dawn most days and tried to help her understand what was happening. At Dawn's request, Cheryl attended Social Services' case review. By the end of the year, Dawn's situation had become more stable (see 'Dawn's story' in Chapter 4) and her relationship with Cheryl had begun to change:

> At the beginning we met like once a week, twice a week and then through the bad times it's been a lot more contact. But recently it's just sort of died off again. She phoned me sort of like said, 'thanks for everything but I don't really need to see you as much now and me life's moved on'.

The Plus element

The young people's attitudes to the Plus element of the programme tended to be very positive. In response to the first follow-up survey, almost all of those who had attended the project indicated that they liked going to Mentoring Plus and that they enjoyed the activities there (92 per cent in both cases). A recurring theme within the depth interviews centred around the idea that, by going to Mentoring Plus, the young people were 'killing two birds with one stone': that is, they were having fun and getting help at the same time:

It's fun to be on the project, cos you do things that are good, it helps you deal with things, helps you with life, they can help you get into college and stuff and you have fun the same time.
(Male young person)

The young people spoke very positively about the project workers. Mentoring Plus was often described in terms of providing a 'relaxed' environment and the project workers were considered to have a key role in this regard. Their non-judgemental approach was contrasted favourably with the reactions of other adults, particularly those, such as teachers, who occupy the role of authority figures. According to one of the young people, the project workers 'treat you like normal people' while another explained:

When you think of a project like this, you would think that it was all people who put their nose up about you because you are all common ... these don't look at you like that, and they think of ways to get you out of trouble. They don't just look at you and think 'oh there's no hope for that person'; like, if you've been arrested or anything like that, they still tell you that you've still got a chance, like they still help you out with trying to get a job and that, but a lot of people would just be like, 'well you've been arrested, you ain't getting the job', so they really help you.
(Young person)

As well as providing practical help, the project workers were considered to have had a therapeutic role as they listened to the young people and talked through problems with them:

It's the best place to go where people listen and do care and they help you get through whatever your troubles are ... and greet you with open arms.
(Male young person)

I love the sort of atmosphere, it is like a little unit. I like units, and I like family feeling ... and they have given so much to me.
(Male young person)

Although the projects were generally described by the young people as providing a supportive environment, much of what they did involved an underlying sense of instability and unpredictability. In private moments, some of the workers expressed serious misgivings about the 'violent', 'intolerant', 'misogynistic' and 'disrespectful' nature of some of the young people's attitudes and behaviour. At the projects, the young people often goaded one another and low-level verbal conflict was commonplace and, although much of this took the form of 'playful' banter, there was a clear potential for escalation. On most occasions, this potential was avoided, as the staff maintained a reasonable degree of control. However, on some occasions, this control broke down and instances of violence and anti-social behaviour were observed by the research team. These incidents occurred most often during the residential.

The residential provides a key early element of the Mentoring Plus programme. Taking the young people away, out of their usual surroundings, is intended to 'build self-awareness and respect, trust in others, cooperation and communication skills' (Benioff, 1997, p. 40). While some of the young people and mentors spoke positively about the residential and described such outcomes, there were clear problems with this element of the programme. Indeed, the extent of the problems we observed suggests that there is something inherently unpredictable about the residential experience. Residentials were characterised by an underlying sense of chaos and tension between the young people and adults (both as project workers and mentors). The young people routinely refused to go to bed at the set time and often kept workers and mentors (and researchers!) up until three or four o'clock in the morning. Among the other challenges that the young people presented were drinking, drug use (mainly cannabis), violence and sexualised behaviour:

> I would go again. It was just mad though, chaos, a weekend where there was just no sleep, and they *[the project workers]* say they are the sex police, and the women patrol the girls' landing and the men patrol the boys' landing … there is no sex, but it is just jumping out of each other's bedroom, you know, and keeping each other apart. But some people want to sleep, so they put the mentors in the bedrooms with us, because the lads crept in, but we weren't doing nothing. We were just sat on the beds talking and then my mate nearly had a fight with one of the lads over something – a packet of crisps or something – so the lads just kept bursting into our room and they broke the door … *[The mentors]* didn't like it. The first ones got out and got another bedroom; the second ones come in and they was all right, they was funny.
> (Young person)

On one residential, a young person attacked another with a pool cue; on another, a group of three young people covered another with toothpaste while he slept and urinated on him; on a third, one of the young people from Mentoring Plus assaulted a young person from another group bursting his eardrum; and, at a fourth, one of the young people became drunk, fell over and injured himself sufficiently that he had to be taken to hospital. In addition, a Mentoring Plus sports day in London ended with a street fight between young people from different projects and the police had to be called.

While residentials are designed to provide an intense experience that breaks down barriers and builds relationships, unintended consequences are produced. Placing a group of young people who are likely to be highly impulsive (Smith and McVie, 2003) in unfamiliar situations with people they do not know appears to constitute a flash point for problematic behaviour. In order to protect the valuable contribution that such events make, the notions of risk and risk assessment should be integrated much more thoroughly into the fabric of the programme.

Conclusions

1   Despite difficulties in implementation, Mentoring Plus achieved relatively high levels of engagement with extremely 'hard to engage' young people.

2   Black and minority ethnic young people were generally well represented on the programme although the low level of South Asian representation is notable.

3   Mentoring cannot be reduced to a simple model, as it contains many elements, phases and stages.

4   The mentoring relationship is difficult to establish and difficult to sustain; it is inherently fragile.

5   Though the 'ideal type' contains an assumption of action towards particular goals (towards substantive work), in practice much mentoring is mundane and reactive.

6   Assumptions about linear development in relationships towards substantive work place significant burdens, and unrealistic expectations, on mentors.

7   While successful relationships were observed between young people and mentor/project workers, the realities of working with this highly disadvantaged group are such that notions of risk and risk management should be at the forefront of programme design and implementation.

4 Impact[1]

Mentoring Plus and the process of change

Mentoring Plus rests on a social deficit model that links offending, truancy and other negative outcomes to social exclusion and disadvantage. A key aim of the programme is to reduce barriers to inclusion by providing access to education, training and work. While this provides a reasonably clear sociological basis for change, psychological dimensions are less well defined. Some elements of the programme did appear to reflect psychological theory and practice: some of the workshops, such as those focusing on smoking cessation and violence/weapons, had significant cognitive-behavioural elements and the role of the mentors was implicitly defined in terms of social learning theory (Bandura, 1977). However, while project staff and mentors talked of role models and of increasing self-esteem and of empowering young people, there was no clear sense of how the young people were expected to change. Mentoring Plus does not work to any clear model of individual change and there is no template of the stages that young people might be expected to go through. Moreover, in some senses, the programme endorses a one-size-fits-all approach. Although the degree of emphasis on each component may have varied according to individual need, the basic structure of the programme was the same for all young people: thus, for example, all those who participated in the programme were expected to have a mentor regardless of whether they wanted one.

Perceived helpfulness of Mentoring Plus

Programme evaluations often employ apparently 'objective' outcome measures with little, if any, consideration of participants' 'subjective' experiences. This, it seems to us, is an important omission. Participants' attitudes towards a programme are likely to be highly suggestive of impact and may act as an important intermediary between implementation and outcome. By the time their involvement in the programme was coming to an end, most of the young people felt that both the Plus element and the mentors had been of some help (see Figure 8).[1] Overall, the Plus element tended to be rated more favourably than the mentors. The proportion of young people who rated the Plus element as 'very helpful' was almost double the proportion who either rated it as 'not at all helpful' or had not engaged with it (45 per cent compared with 23 per cent). A greater degree of ambivalence was evident in relation to the mentors, as the proportion who rated them as 'very helpful' was only slightly larger than the proportion who either rated them 'not at all helpful' or had not engaged with them (37 per cent compared with 30 per cent). Moreover, although levels of non-engagement were very similar for both components, the mentors were rated as 'not at all helpful' at almost twice the rate of the Plus element. Judgements about helpfulness appeared to be fairly robust and were generally unchanged some six months after the programme had come to an end.

Figure 8 Young people's assessment of Mentoring Plus and their mentors (per cent in cohort)

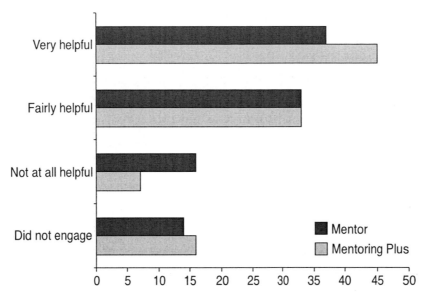

Source: Mentoring Plus cohort (first follow-up survey).
n = 195.

Crucially, these judgements varied markedly across the projects. The proportion of young people who rated the Plus element as 'very helpful' varied from approximately two in three (63 per cent) to one in four (25 per cent); while a similar degree of variation was evident in relation to the mentors (58 per cent to 27 per cent). The ratings of the individual projects on these different dimensions were highly consistent, with those that were rated most highly in relation to the Plus element tending also to be rated most highly in relation to the mentors.[2] Overall judgements about the helpfulness of the programme[3] were linked to the integrity with which they were implemented, with the key distinction being between projects that achieved a high or moderate level of integrity and those that did not. Participants in projects that were highly or moderately well implemented were one-and-a-half times as likely as those in poorly implemented projects to rate the programme as 'very helpful' (62 per cent, 60 per cent and 40 per cent respectively).[4]

As well as providing general assessments of how helpful the programme had been, the young people who responded to the follow-up surveys were asked to indicate how, or in which areas, the programme had helped them. The most frequently identified areas of help were those connected to general functioning such as goal setting, self-confidence and decision making (see Figure 9). In terms of social exclusion, the programme was thought to have been most helpful in relation to education and somewhat less so in relation to work and offending:

When we first met up we had to write my CV and sort out my hostel and we did that and then I got a job for the summer, she sorted out all my school cause I weren't going to school and didn't go in for all my exams, and so she sorted that out for me ... She's just helped me feel more organised, basically, I've told her what I want to do, and she just helped me to do it, and she's been there to push me the few steps I've needed to be pushed ... If she weren't there I wouldn't be going back to school. I used to go and hang around the streets and do crime and stuff but now I can't be bothered to do that because I want to get a job, just want to go to college.
(Young person)

In my last school I was really, really bad and I got excluded four times ... *[for]* hitting a teacher with a chair, punching a teacher in the head, fighting and throwing a chair through the window ... I had a bad temper problem and I couldn't control it ... I normally meet Janine *[mentor]* every Tuesday or Wednesday or Monday to talk to see what I have done at school, I show her the work, what I done and then we talk ... *[Mentors]* help you control your temper and they take you out places and it helps you in school because they give you targets and that helps you get merits and smiles – so it gives you targets to do.
(Young person)

Figure 9 Areas in which the programme was considered to have been helpful (per cent in cohort)

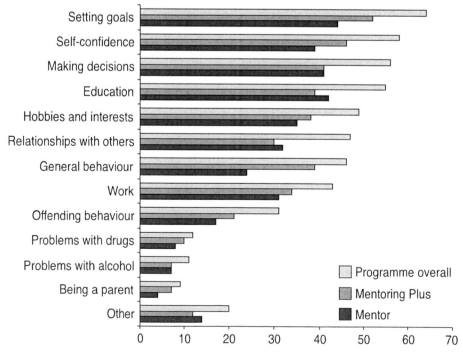

Source: Mentoring Plus cohort (first follow-up survey).
n = 189.

While the Plus element of the programme tended to be rated as more helpful than the mentors, there were a few exceptions to this general trend. Most notably, the number of young people who indicated that their mentor had helped them in the areas of education and work was almost the same as the number who indicated that they had been helped by the Plus element in these areas. In part, this reflected the way in which the two elements of the programme tended to complement one another. The proportion of young people who indicated that they had been helped by either element of the programme tended not to be very much greater than the proportion who indicated that they had been helped by either the mentors or the Plus element. And it follows from this that, in most cases, the young people had been helped by both elements rather than by one of them in isolation:

> My young mentee, it's helped her a lot and I think it's the education programme that's made her realise that 'yeah I can do things', you know it's got her confidence as well. Every now and again we like sit down on a one-to-one and do the work together … She's gained entry level one in Maths and English and we talked about level two and it was 'no, I'm not doing that, that's too hard'. Like at the presentation the other evening she picked up four certificates and I said to her 'I'm really proud, are you glad you did it now?' and she went 'yeah I'm glad'. And I said to her jokingly, 'well, we'll start that level two soon' and she went 'no', but the next day she was on the phone, 'I want to start level two, will you come and help me?' (Mentor)

Changing circumstances?

A substantial proportion of the young people recruited to Mentoring Plus felt that the programme had helped them in some way and it is crucial to consider whether these subjective assessments were matched by changes in their objective circumstances. The potential impact of the programme was assessed in relation to engagement with education, training and work, family relationships, offending, substance use and self-esteem. For each of these areas, we consider whether any changes were evident among the young people in the cohort during the course of the programme and in the six months that followed, before going on to compare the profile of programme participants and non-participants.

We noted earlier that levels of engagement in Mentoring Plus varied according to the young people's demographic characteristics (see Chapter 3) and it is important to assess the implications that this may have in relation to impact. If the profiles of the two groups vary markedly from one another, then it may be that it is these variations, rather than participation in the programme, that explain any differences in outcome. A breakdown of the key demographic characteristics for programme participants and non-participants is shown in Table 6.

Table 6 Demographic characteristics of programme participants and non-participants (per cent)[a]

	Participants	Non-participants
Age		
12–14	17	15
15	48	47
16	21	23
17–19	14	16
	100	*100*
Sex		
Male	65	72
Female	35	28
	100	*100*
Ethnicity		
White	39	53
Black African/Caribbean	46	30
Asian	2	10
Mixed race/dual heritage	13	7
	100	*100*

Source: Mentoring Plus cohort (first survey).

n = 164 (participants); 70 (non-participants). Percentages do not always add to 100 due to rounding.

a   The figures given here are based on the young people who responded to both the initial survey and the first follow-up.

Crucially, the age profiles of the two groups were very similar. This was particularly important, as our key outcome indicators, such as engagement in education, training and work, offending and substance use, vary markedly with age. Although the sex and ethnicity profiles of participants and non-participants differed, this arguably had less serious implications for measuring impact. At the start of the programme, the key outcome indicators tended to vary more markedly with age than with either ethnicity or sex.

Education, training and work

Important changes were evident in the current status of the young people who joined Mentoring Plus during the year of the programme and, in many ways, these changes reflected the transition through adolescence and into early adulthood (see Figure 10).[5] The biggest shift appeared to be from school to college/university, as the proportion of young people in the cohort who were, or should have been, in school almost halved while the proportion in college/university more than tripled. Large relative increases were also evident in relation to training schemes and paid work, although the numbers involved in these activities remained fairly small.

Figure 10 Main activity at the beginning and end of the programme (per cent in cohort)

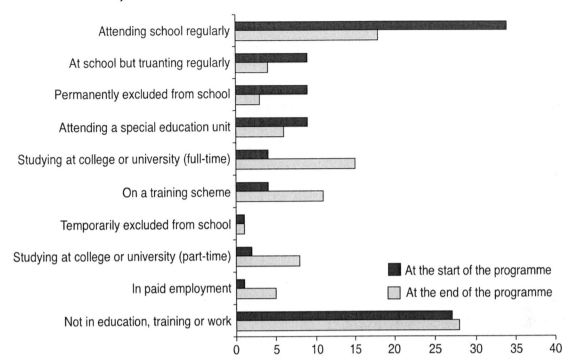

Source: Mentoring Plus cohort (original survey and first follow-up).
n = 167.
Note: the figures given here are based on members of the cohort who responded to both the original questionnaire and the first follow-up.

Crucially, the proportion of young people who appeared to be completely disengaged from education, training and work remained largely the same, although, if we combine this category with those who were truanting regularly or were excluded from school, there was, arguably, some overall improvement in the position of the young people who joined the programme (the proportion in these categories fell from 46 to 36 per cent).

As they moved from school to college, training and work, a reasonably large number of the young people who joined Mentoring Plus secured formal qualifications. During the year they were involved in the programme, one in four (27 per cent) gained GCSEs, one in 12 (8 per cent) gained an NVQ and one in 20 (5 per cent) gained a BTEC or City and Guilds qualification. And, in the six months that followed the end of the programme, one in seven (15 per cent) gained GCSEs, one in ten (9 per cent) gained an NVQ and one in 33 (3 per cent) gained a BTEC or City and Guilds qualification.

Further changes were evident by the time of the second, 18-month, follow-up, primarily in relation to school and paid work. The proportion of the cohort in paid work more than doubled by this time to one in eight (13 per cent); while the proportion who were, or should have been, attending school fell to below one in four (17 per cent were at school, less than 1 per cent were temporarily excluded from school and 3 per cent were attending a special education unit).[6] In contrast, the numbers of young people who were studying at college or university (18 per cent full time and 8 per cent part time) or were on a training scheme (9 per cent) remained largely unchanged, as did the proportion who were disengaged from education, training and work (32 per cent).

To assess whether any of these changes in current status might reasonably be attributed to Mentoring Plus, the young people who had participated in the programme were compared with those who had not.[7] Given that education and work were two of the areas in which the mentors and the Plus element of the programme appeared to be most helpful to the young people, we may expect to see some evidence of impact here.

At the time of the first survey, programme participants and non-participants shared a broadly similar profile, although the former appeared to be somewhat more disaffected (see Table 7). While there was very little difference in the proportion of these groups who were in paid work or on a training scheme, non-participants were more likely to be attending school or a special education unit, or to be studying at college or university. As many as one in two (51 per cent) of the participants were excluded from school, regularly truanting or completely disengaged from education, employment and training, and this compared with less than one in three (31 per cent) of non-participants.

By the end of the programme, however, this gap had all but closed (38 per cent of participants and 33 per cent of non-participants were in such a position). The proportion of participants and non-participants attending school or a special education unit fell and this trend was particularly marked in relation to participants (the percentage of participants in this category fell by 17 points compared with nine points among non-participants). Differences in relation to school, however, were more than offset by differences in relation to college/university, training schemes and paid work, and it was through these activities that participants in the programme reduced their rate of disengagement relative to non-participants. Crucially, while the proportion of participants who were not in education, employment or training fell slightly during the course of the programme, this coincided with a quite marked increase in the proportion of non-participants who were in this position.

Table 7 Main activity at the beginning and end of the programme by participation (per cent)

	Beginning of programme	End of programme	Change
Participants			
Attending school/special education unit	38	21	−17
Studying at college or university	6	25	+19
On a training scheme or in paid employment	6	17	+11
At school but truanting regularly	10 ⎫	5 ⎫	−5 ⎫
Excluded from school	11 ⎬ 51	5 ⎬ 38	−6 ⎬ −13
Not in education, employment or training	30 ⎭	28 ⎭	−2 ⎭
	100	100	
Non-participants			
Attending school/special education unit	47	38	−9
Studying at college or university	15	18	+3
On a training scheme or in paid employment	7	12	+5
At school but truanting regularly	7 ⎫	1 ⎫	−6 ⎫
Excluded from school	4 ⎬ 31	0 ⎬ 33	−4 ⎬ +2
Not in education, employment or training	20 ⎭	32 ⎭	+12 ⎭
	100	100	

Source: Mentoring Plus cohort (original survey and first follow-up).

n = 152 (participants); 67 (non-participants).

Note: the figures given here are based on individuals who responded to both the original questionnaire and the first follow-up. Percentages do not always add to 100 due to rounding.

These changes in activity may be thought of in terms of movement between social inclusion and exclusion. For the purposes of this analysis, attending school or a special education unit, studying at college/university, training and paid work were defined as states of social inclusion while truanting regularly, school exclusion and disengagement from employment, education and training were considered to be states of social exclusion. A smaller proportion of participants than non-participants maintained a position of social inclusion during the course of the programme and a larger proportion maintained a position of social exclusion (see Figure 11). To some extent, this simply reflected the situation at the start of the programme, as participants were less likely to have been in a position of social inclusion at this point.

Among non-participants, considerable continuity was evident in the balance between inclusion and exclusion during the period covered by the programme, as movements between these categories cancelled each other out (the proportion of non-participants who were in a position of inclusion fell slightly from 69 to 67 per cent). Among programme participants, in contrast, there was a marked increase in social inclusion. Almost twice as many participants moved from positions of exclusion to inclusion as moved from positions of inclusion to exclusion and, between the start and end of the programme, the number in positions of inclusion increased by more

Figure 11 Movement between inclusion and exclusion (per cent of participants and non-participants)

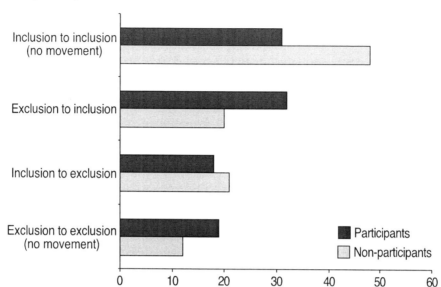

Source: Mentoring Plus cohort and comparison group (original survey and first follow-up).
$n = 152$ (participants); 67 (non-participants).
Note: the figures given here are based on individuals who responded to both the original
questionnaire and the first follow-up.

than a quarter (from 49 to 63 per cent).[8] Three-fifths (59 per cent) of the participants
who were disengaged from education, employment and training at the start of the
programme were either attending college or university by the end of the programme,
or were on a training scheme or in paid work and this constituted the key movement
within this group.

The differences between participants and non-participants suggest that the
programme had a positive effect on rates of social inclusion. There were, moreover,
further indications that Mentoring Plus played an important role in bringing about the
positive changes that were evident among programme participants. Nearly three in
four (73 per cent) of the participants who moved from a position of exclusion into a
position of inclusion noted that their mentor or the Plus component had helped them
in relation to education and/or work. Two in three (66 per cent) indicated that they
had been helped by their mentor and three in five (60 per cent) indicated that they
had been helped by the Plus component. A strong degree of overlap was evident
here, as the vast majority of those who had been helped by their mentor had also
been helped by the Plus element and vice versa (76 per cent and 83 per cent
respectively).

In addition, the apparent impact of the programme varied across the projects and was greatest in those that had the highest level of programme integrity. In one of the projects, fewer participants were in a position of inclusion at the end of the programme than at the start (38 per cent compared with 63 per cent) while, among the remaining projects, rates of inclusion increased by between one-tenth to more than two-thirds (from 9 per cent to 70 per cent). These differences were clearly linked to the integrity with which the programme was implemented (see Table 8). For projects with a low level of programme integrity, the balance between inclusion and exclusion remained unchanged while, for those with a moderate or high level of integrity, rates of inclusion increased by a third (34 per cent) and two-fifths (41 per cent) respectively.[9]

Table 8 Changing rates of inclusion among participants by programme integrity (per cent)

| Level of programme integrity | Proportion of participants in positions of inclusion ... | | | |
	At the beginning of the programme	At the end of the programme	Change	n
High	46	65	+19	81
Moderate	53	71	+18	41
Low	52	52	0	30

Source: Mentoring Plus cohort (original survey and first follow-up).
Note: the figures given here are based on individuals who responded to both the original questionnaire and the first follow-up.

Case study: Gary's story

Gary was 18 years old when he joined Mentoring Plus and was living in a hostel around the corner from the project. It was the fifth hostel he had lived in since being 'kicked out' by his stepfather some months earlier. He said he was 'happy' with this hostel, as it was not like the 'disgusting, nasty hostels' he had lived in previously.

Before joining Mentoring Plus, Gary had been involved in 'all sorts of crime' – stealing cars, stealing mobile phones and 'craziness like that'. Thinking back to that time, he described himself as a 'street rat'. Gary said he had got involved in crime because everybody he knew was doing robberies and because he wanted to fit in with the people he was hanging around with. Unlike his friends, Gary had grown up in a 'posh area' and described himself as a 'posh bloke' but felt he had had to change in order to fit in.

(Continued overleaf)

Gary joined Mentoring Plus when his cousin told him he was going on to the programme. At that time, Gary was in 'a bit of trouble' and felt 'any help would have been appreciated at that time so I just took it up'. Over the course of the year, he was in regular contact with his mentor and the project workers, who he saw as being more like mentors. He got involved with the music workshop, helped teach the other young people mixing, etc. and completed a community work course.

By the time we interviewed Gary, he had got a 'well paid job' as a sports community worker and had another one 'lined up'. He felt that everything was going smoothly for him and, even though he was financially less well off than before, he said he would not go back to his old lifestyle: 'there's nothing there for me any more. It's not fun any more, it's just boring and I've grown out of it now.' Gary said that Mentoring Plus had played an important role in bringing about this change.

> It was because I was bored that I was doing the crimes or whatever I was doing, so whenever I was bored I would just come here and talk to the people in the project or talk to my mentor and they would just show me different ways to get a job, go out and study, I mean they put me on different courses that I've done … There's things that you can talk to your mentor about that sometimes you can't talk to your friends about and knowing that they are your mentor and they have got that adult responsibility whereas my friends would probably have just laughed at the things I would have told them.

Without the project, Gary felt he would not have got his job 'because I've got no experience, I would have never have even thought about doing anything like that before, but doing it showed me a lot of things that I can do now'.

Case study: Dawn's story

Dawn was 16 years old when she joined Mentoring Plus and had been living in care for two years. Prior to this, she had lived with her mum but they argued all the time and, following a fight, they both decided that it 'was best if I went away. It was only meant to be for one night to sort my head out, but then it was a month and then a year and it just went on.' Dawn spent a lot of time on her own and described her life as 'boring'.

(Continued)

Dawn had been referred to Mentoring Plus by an Education Welfare Officer who was concerned that she was not attending school. Dawn was told that Mentoring Plus was 'not like mainstream school' and that, while she could not do her GCSEs there, she could do some maths, English and computer work. Dawn didn't mind about the GCSEs, as she said she had not wanted to do them anyway.

Although she was a little nervous about going to Mentoring Plus, she went to see what it was like. She felt that the young people at the project were in the same situation as her and described Mentoring Plus as being better than school: 'It's better than school because they treat you like an adult whereas at school they treat you like kids, so it's good like that'. She attended the project three times a week and participated in the education workshops, the girls' group and social events. She also met regularly with her mentor.

Dawn met Cheryl, her mentor, on the residential. She had chosen two mentors and said she wasn't bothered who she was matched with. Although she knew that she was going to get a mentor, Dawn didn't know what to expect as 'it was all new'. Dawn and Cheryl met 'all the time'; they would meet at McDonald's or Burger King to chat and eat. Dawn liked meeting with her mentor and appreciated the way that Cheryl did not 'push her into things' she did not want to do. When they first met, Dawn wanted to be a hairdresser and Cheryl helped her enrol on a hairdressing course. Dawn did not like it, however, and left, saying she was glad that Cheryl had not judged her. Dawn felt Cheryl was there for her 'at anytime' and would call her 'dead late in the night' when she needed help. Although Dawn thought her mother 'would probably be there for her', she felt more comfortable calling Cheryl.

Dawn believed that the main benefit she had gained from being involved with Mentoring Plus was that it had helped increase her confidence: 'it has helped me with my self-confidence and that because before I came I didn't have no confidence about myself and it has helped me with my confidence'. Dawn gained certificates for maths and English through Mentoring Plus. At the time of the interview, she was studying a health and social care course at college and was enjoying it.

Family

The family contexts within which the young people were living remained largely unchanged during the period covered by the programme. The vast majority (74 per cent) of the cohort were living in the same family structure at the end of the programme as at the beginning and, although a fairly large proportion indicated that the programme had helped to improve their relationships with others, there was little evidence of increased family attachment.[10] The proportion showing strong family attachment remained largely unchanged (16 per cent and 19 per cent respectively) as did the proportion showing moderate attachment (69 per cent and 65 per cent respectively) and weak attachment (16 per cent and 17 per cent respectively). There was, however, some evidence of moderately improved relationships during the aftermath of the programme, as three-quarters (77 per cent) of those who showed weak family attachment at the end of the programme showed moderate attachment six months later. By this stage, the proportion of the cohort showing weak family attachment had fallen to below one in ten (9 per cent).

There was little suggestion that these modest improvements in family relationships were due to participation in Mentoring Plus. During the lifetime of the programme, the balance between strong and weak family attachment remained largely unchanged among both participants and non-participants.

Offending

At the start of the programme, most of the young people who were recruited to Mentoring Plus had yet to reach the age at which we might expect to see substantial reductions in their offending and there was little, if any, suggestion that they were 'growing out' of crime. The vast majority had offended during the 12 months leading up to the start of the programme and many had done so persistently (see Chapter 2). Nevertheless, a sizeable proportion of these young people indicated that Mentoring Plus had helped to tackle their offending. And further analyses confirmed that fairly substantial reductions in offending were evident during the lifetime of the programme. In assessing the following evidence, it is important to remember that participation in the programme was voluntary and that referrals tended to focus on young people for whom it was thought to be appropriate. Thus, those who were referred to, and/or who participated in, the programme may have differed from the wider offending population in important ways. Certainly, a large proportion of them indicated that they had joined the programme because they had wanted to stop getting into trouble.

On average, members of the cohort reported having committed only one of the listed offences during the 12 months covered by the programme, which was two less than in the previous 12 months. By the end of the programme, more than one in four (29 per cent) indicated that they had not offended in the previous 12 months and this represented an increase of almost two-thirds compared with the start of the programme (18 per cent). The vast majority of those who had offended in the 12 months leading up to the programme either stopped doing so or continued at a reduced rate (30 per cent and 43 per cent respectively; 8 per cent reported no change while 19 per cent reported an increased rate of offending). The general downturn in offending was particularly marked among members of the cohort who had offended persistently in the year before the programme as, on average, they went on to commit four fewer offence types during the following year. As a result, the number of persistent offenders fell by more than a third (from 58 per cent to 37 per cent).

Based on levels of offending in the general population, we may expect to see the greatest reduction in criminal damage, as young people are most likely to 'grow out' of this type of crime. With the exception of traffic violations, however, fairly substantial reductions were evident across the range of offence categories. The greatest proportionate decrease was evident in relation to violence, with the number of young people committing such offences during the previous 12 months falling by almost two-fifths (from 62 to 35 per cent). Fairly substantial reductions were also evident in relation to criminal damage (from 53 to 34 per cent) and property crimes (from 55 to 43 per cent). The number committing traffic violations, by contrast, remained stable (35 compared with 37 per cent).

These general patterns were confirmed by analysis of more specific offences (see Figure 12). The greatest proportionate reduction was evident in relation to carrying a weapon to attack somebody (the numbers committing such an offence in the previous 12 months fell by three-fifths or 60 per cent)[11] while other violent offences such as beating somebody up, fighting in a public place and hurting somebody with a weapon were also subject to fairly substantial decreases. More moderate reductions tended to be apparent in relation to acts of criminal damage and property offences while the rate at which traffic violations were committed remained largely unchanged.

Figure 12 Levels of offending at the start and end of the programme (per cent in cohort)

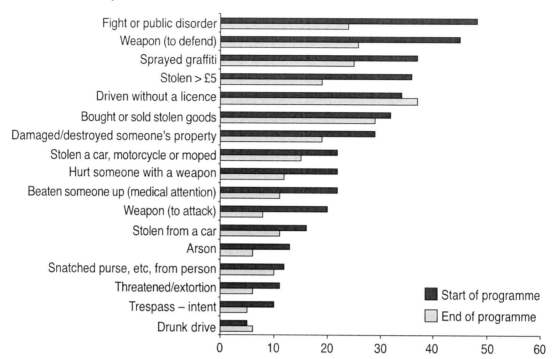

Source: Mentoring Plus cohort (original survey and first follow-up).
n = 168.
Note: the figures given here are based on individuals who responded to both the original questionnaire and the first follow-up.

The reduced levels of offending that were evident during the lifetime of the programme were more than maintained in the six months that followed.[12] The vast majority (83 per cent) of young people who had not offended while the programme was in place continued not to do so once it had come to an end. Added to this, one in three (34 per cent) of those who had committed an offence while the programme was running refrained from doing so in the following period. Furthermore, those who continued to offend did so at a relatively moderate rate, committing an average of two of the listed offences, which was one less than in the previous 12 months and three less than in the 12 months before that. Consequently, while the proportion of non-offenders increased to almost one in two (45 per cent) following the end of the programme the proportion of persistent offenders fell to one in four (26 per cent).

Although these reductions in offending were consistent with the aims of Mentoring Plus, they cannot be attributed directly to the programme. Participants and non-participants showed similar levels of offending at the outset of the programme and, while fairly substantial subsequent reductions were evident among programme participants, similar, and in some cases more marked, reductions were reported by non-participants (see Table 9).

Table 9 Offending by participation in Mentoring Plus – general measures

Participated in Mentoring Plus?	Offended (%)		Offended persistently (%)		Median no. of offences		n
	Year one	Year two	Year one	Year two	Year one	Year two	
Yes	82	71	58	39	3	2	155
No	84	62	53	37	3	1	68

Source: Mentoring Plus cohort and comparison group (original survey and first follow-up).
Notes: The figures given here are based on individuals who responded to both the original questionnaire and the first follow-up.
Year one = 12 months prior to programme; Year two = 12 months covered by programme.

This general pattern was replicated in relation to specific offences, as the largest proportionate reductions tended to be evident among non-participants. Closer scrutiny of the changes that were apparent among programme participants reinforced the conclusion that reductions in offending could not be attributed with any confidence to the programme. Inconsistencies were evident across the projects, which could not be readily explained either by the content of the programme or by the integrity of the implementation: crucially, reductions in offending were evident, regardless of how well the programme had been implemented.[13] Moreover, while the social deficit model underpinning Mentoring Plus suggests that reductions in offending should have been most marked among participants who moved from positions of social exclusion to inclusion, no such pattern was evident. Indeed, during the course of the programme and the six months that followed, the greatest reductions were evident among those who continued to be socially excluded.[14] It remains possible, however, that the increased rates of inclusion associated with participation in the programme will have a positive impact on levels of offending over a longer period of time.

Finally, those participants who indicated that the programme had helped to tackle their offending behaviour did not show particularly marked reductions in actual offending. The proportion of these participants who reported having offended in the previous 12 months did not change between the start and end of the programme; and the proportion who offended persistently fell by a very modest amount (from 68 to 58 per cent). During the course of the programme, a much more marked reduction in persistent offending was evident among those who did not indicate that the programme had helped to tackle their offending behaviour (the proportion of persistent offenders in this group fell from 53 to 26 per cent). In the six months that followed, however, the proportion of persistent offenders within these groups converged (19 per cent of both groups offended persistently). And, over this extended period, the proportion of persistent offenders fell by approximately two-thirds regardless of whether or not they indicated that the programme had helped to tackle their offending behaviour.[15]

Drinking, smoking and drug use

Levels of smoking within the cohort remained very consistent throughout the period covered by the study. The proportion of participants who were smoking on a daily basis remained largely unchanged from the beginning to the end and to six months after the programme (45 per cent, 50 per cent and 44 per cent respectively). And a similar degree of stability was evident in relation to the proportion of non-smokers (42 per cent, 38 per cent and 42 per cent). This general pattern reflected the persistent nature of individuals' smoking habits, as most of those who were smoking regularly at the start of the programme were still doing so 12 months and 18 months later, and most non-smokers continued not to smoke. The changes that were evident during the lifetime of the programme were similar among participants and non-participants, and thus it appeared that the programme had little, if any, impact on smoking.[16]

In contrast to the stability that was evident in relation to smoking, drinking and drunkenness became more widespread within the cohort during the lifetime of the study (see Figure 13). Between the start and end of the programme, the proportion of young people who drank alcohol on a weekly basis increased from one in seven to one in five, and six months later it had increased to one in four. During the same period, the proportion who did not drink at all fell by almost a half from more than one in four to less than one in seven. Of those who started out as non-drinkers, slightly more than half (55 per cent) had started to drink by the end of the programme and more than three in four (68 per cent) had done so six months later. In relation to drunkenness, there was a clear trend towards polarisation, as the proportion getting drunk frequently and the proportion who did not get drunk at all increased simultaneously. Infrequent drunkenness became markedly less common as the young people in this category either stopped getting drunk or became drunk more often: a quarter (28 per cent) of those who were getting drunk less than once a week at the start of the programme were doing so more often by the end of the programme and one in three (36 per cent) were no longer getting drunk at all.

Given the age of the young people involved in Mentoring Plus, the changes that were evident in their consumption of alcohol are unsurprising. The mid-to-late teens constitute a key phase in drinking transitions as young people learn increasingly to drink like adults (Newburn and Shiner, 2001). And comparisons with non-participants in the programme indicated that there was nothing remarkable in the way drinking patterns changed among participants, many of whom continued to drink moderately. Between the start and end of the programme, the proportion of participants and non-participants who did not drink fell by approximately a quarter (from 25 to 18 per cent and from 32 to 24 per cent respectively) and the proportion that got drunk on a weekly basis doubled (from 6 to 11

Figure 13 Drinking and drunkenness in the cohort (per cent in the cohort)

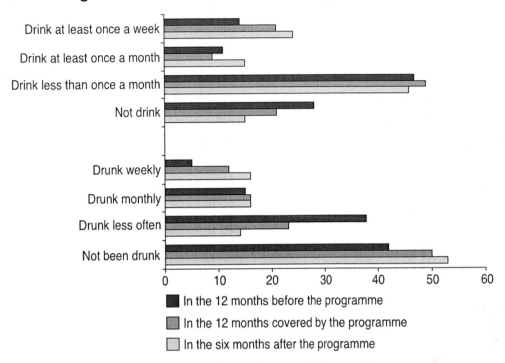

Source: Mentoring Plus cohort (first survey; first and second follow-up).
n = 170 (12 months before the programme and 12 months covered by the programme)
n = 108 (six months following the programme).
Note: figures given here for the 12 months before the programme and the 12 months covered by the programme are based on individuals who responded to both the original questionnaire and the first follow-up.

per cent and from 6 to 13 per cent respectively). Equally, however, approximately half of the young people in both groups did not get drunk during the 12 months covered by the programme (46 per cent and 56 per cent respectively).[17]

The mid-to-late teens also constitute a key period of change in relation to illicit drugs as levels of use tend to increase sharply. To some extent, this was reflected in the cohort as one in three (33 per cent) of the young people who had not used drugs during the 12 months prior to the programme did so in the following year. This apparent movement into drug use was offset, however, by movements the other way: while one in eight of the young people in the cohort started to use drugs during the period covered by the programme, an almost identical number stopped doing so (13 per cent and 12 per cent respectively). Alongside these changes, there was considerable stability. Most of the young people who had used drugs in the year before the programme continued to do so in the following year (81 per cent) and most of those who had not done so continued not to (67 per cent).[18] Crucially, as movements into and out of illicit drug use cancelled each other out, there was very little change in overall levels of use (see Figure 14).

Figure 14 Illicit drug use in the cohort (per cent in the cohort)

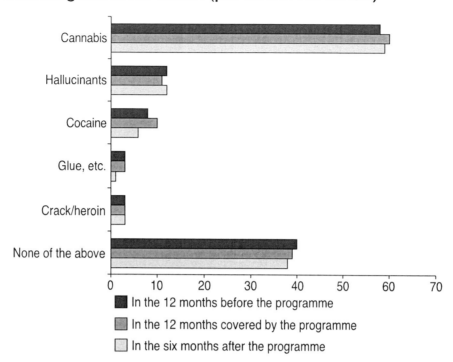

In the 12 months before the programme
In the 12 months covered by the programme
In the six months after the programme

Source: Mentoring Plus cohort (first survey; first and second follow-up).
n = 162 (12 months before the programme and 12 months covered by the programme).
n = 101 (six months following the programme).
Note: figures given here for the 12 months before the programme and the 12 months covered by the programme are based on individuals who responded to both the original questionnaire and the first follow-up.

This high degree of consistency suggests that the programme had very little, if any, impact on participants' use of illicit drugs and comparisons with non-participants confirmed this conclusion. At the start of the programme, drug use was more widespread among participants than non-participants. Almost two in five (39 per cent) participants had used cannabis on a weekly basis during the previous 12 months compared with one in four (26 per cent) non-participants, for example, and slightly more than one in ten (11 per cent) had used cocaine in this period compared with none of the non-participants. These differences continued to be evident during the period covered by the programme as overall levels of use remained very stable among both participants and non-participants.[19]

Self-esteem

As we have argued, self-esteem is central to the discourse surrounding mentoring and the young people's assessments of Mentoring Plus implied that the greatest impact might have been made in these areas. While there was evidence that some of the young people's self-esteem improved during the course of the programme, this evidence was limited to a discrete sub-group within the cohort and was not part

66

of a general trend. Overall levels of self-esteem within the cohort remained largely unchanged throughout the study (the average score varied by one point from the start of the programme to six months after it had come to an end).

Changes in self-esteem varied according to how the young people felt about themselves at the start of the programme. Those who had the poorest self-image at the outset were the most likely to say that Mentoring Plus had helped their self-confidence and this was reflected in relation to actual changes in self-esteem. For those members of the cohort whose self-esteem was very or moderately high at the start of the programme,[20] there was very little evidence of change (see Table 10). For those whose self-esteem was very or moderately low, however, there was clear improvement over the course of the programme, which was maintained during the six months that followed.

It is unclear whether or not these changes can be attributed to Mentoring Plus. On the one hand, those young people who indicated that Mentoring Plus had helped to improve their confidence recorded improved self-esteem scores: on average, their score improved by two points during the course of the programme and this compared with a slight worsening of half a point for those who indicated that they had received no such help. On the other hand, improvements in self-esteem were not limited to those young people who participated in the programme. Indeed, the self-esteem profiles of participants and non-participants were very similar and those young people who had relatively low self-esteem at the outset recorded very similar rates of improvement regardless of whether or not they took part in the programme. Among those who started out with very low self esteem, the average score improved by four points for both participants and non-participants (from 27 to 23 and from 26

Table 10 Self esteem (average score within the cohort)[a]

	Start of programme	End of programme	Six months later
Self-esteem at start of programme ...			
Very high	16	16	17
Moderately high	20	19	20
Moderately low	23	21	20
Very low	27	23	22

Source: Mentoring Plus cohort (first survey; first and second follow-up).

n = 156 (first survey and first follow-up).

n = 96 (second follow-up).

Notes:

The figures given here for the start and end of this programme, are based on individuals who responded to both the original questionnaire and the first follow-up.

Scores on this scale could vary between 10 and 40, low scores indicated high self-esteem and high scores indicated low self-esteem.

a We used Rosenberg's (1965) scale to measure self-esteem. For information on this scale, please refer to Appendix 2.

to 22 respectively). On balance, it seems likely that Mentoring Plus helped to enhance the self-esteem of those participants who had a poor self-image, while non-participants with a poor self-image found similar help/support elsewhere.

Case study: Karen's story

At the time of her first interview, Karen was living with her 'auntie'. She did not get on with her father and was missing her mother who was living abroad with her boyfriend and Karen's little brother and sister:

> It is horrible, I miss my mum … Sometimes I just cry and I think I wish I had my mum because I am at that age now where I want to talk to my mum … and I haven't got that and it is really like horrible … I used to wake up in the morning and every morning 'morning mum, good night mum', and now it is just like I don't use the word mum no more, and it is horrible.

Karen was feeling unhappy living with her auntie, who she felt was favouring her own children. Karen spent most of her time at home by herself, as she had been excluded from school. At night, she used to 'hang out' with a group of older boys and felt it was fun until people started to 'call me names and call me a slag':

> It made me feel upset, depressed, had like low self-confidence and every time I used to go out and I used to just look at people and think 'why are they looking at me?', and I used to get paranoid, 'do they think I am a whore?' and I used to get paranoid.

Karen felt that Mentoring Plus, in particular the girls' nights she used to participate in on a regular basis, helped her think more positively about herself and her relationship with her mother. Further, she felt that the project helped her be more confident when dealing with other people, especially young men. At the time of her second interview, Karen did not 'hang out' with older boys any more but was mixing more with young people her own age:

> Girls' night – it's really just a couple of girls and some workers and we go upstairs and we talk about self-esteem, self-respect and them kind of things, and it's good because it helps you to understand certain things about yourself and how to deal with certain things, like if you're walking down the road and a boy comes up to you – he looks threatening and he asks you for your number – don't say yes just because he looks threatening; just say no, speak your mind.

(Continued)

With regard to her mother, Karen said:

> I never used to cope with it very well – I used to run away from home and
> do bodily harm and you know, try and just get away from it all, but now I just
> think about it, but I try not to think about it the way I used to and think that it
> is all bad – maybe it isn't all bad and maybe something good can come out
> of it – so I just try and push past it and move on.

Overall, she felt that Mentoring Plus had been very helpful, especially in terms of
raising her self-esteem:

> Before I came to Mentoring Plus, I had very low self-esteem and I didn't
> have no confidence. Mentoring Plus helped me – by the time I had finished,
> my self-esteem had gone up. I wouldn't say I have untold self-esteem, but
> my self-esteem had gone up and I felt more certain … sure about myself.

Conclusions

1   The analysis presented in this chapter challenges the old orthodoxy that 'nothing
    works'. Fairly substantial changes were evident among the young people referred
    to Mentoring Plus during the lifetime of the programme, particularly in relation to
    rates of social inclusion and levels of offending. It is important to remember,
    however, that referrals to the programme focused on young people for whom it
    was thought to be appropriate and that participation in the programme was
    voluntary.

2   Not all of the changes that were evident among young people could be attributed
    to participation in Mentoring Plus and variations in this regard highlighted the
    importance of programme integrity.

3   Mentoring Plus appeared to have greatest impact in relation to social exclusion/
    inclusion, which is perhaps unsurprising, as it is here that the methods of the
    programme relate most clearly to the aims. Such impact was most apparent in
    projects that were implemented reasonably or very well.

4   There was little structured work that related directly to the other aims of the
    programme. There was, for example, no explicit focus on challenging offending
    behaviour. Moreover, within the Mentoring Plus programme, the model of
    'change' is largely implicit rather than explicit and, where it is made explicit, it
    tends to be generalised rather than specific or targeted.

5   In so far as Mentoring Plus seeks to reduce offending, it does so indirectly by reducing the barriers to social inclusion. However, the gains that were evident in relation to social inclusion did not translate into reductions in offending during the period covered by the evaluation, although it remains possible that they will do so over a more extended period.

6   Although levels of offending did fall fairly substantially among the young people who participated in Mentoring Plus, similar, and in some cases more marked, reductions were evident among non-participants.

7   In general, the young people felt that the Plus component had been more helpful than the mentors. In those areas where the programme appeared to have had most impact (i.e. education and work), however, the mentors were rated as having been as helpful as the Plus component.

5 Conclusions

This research challenges the old – admittedly mistaken – adage that 'nothing works'. It shows that positive interventions can be made that help to bring about fairly substantial changes in the lives of even the most highly disaffected young people. Mentoring Plus, which provided the focus for the research, recruited and engaged actively with a large number of young people who were at considerable risk of social exclusion (including a large proportion from black African/Caribbean communities). Most importantly, perhaps, it was also reasonably successful in encouraging these young people to (re)engage with education and work. And the related benefits of the programme, in terms of social inclusion, may be both significant and far-reaching.

These achievements are all the more impressive when they are set in context. Interventions with disaffected young people are inherently difficult to implement and these difficulties are exacerbated markedly by a climate of insecure funding, fixed-term employment and high staff turnover. Delivering a consistent and coherent service under such circumstances is far from straightforward, and this study adds to the significant body of research that shows that implementation failure – or at least inadequate implementation – often lies at the heart of the inability to deliver better outcomes. While many of the Mentoring Plus projects ran into operational difficulties, those that achieved a reasonable level of programme integrity had the greatest impact in terms of encouraging young people (back) into education and work. It follows that, in a more secure environment, the overall impact of the programme would have been greater and it therefore behoves policy makers and funders to think carefully about how they support such programmes in the future. All too often, it appears, potentially positive work with young people is compromised by circumstances that serve to undermine, or at least limit, programme integrity.

In terms of future development, however, mentoring does not simply require more secure and longer-term funding. There is also a need to think more fully through the details of the process. The impact that Mentoring Plus had on the young people who took part in the programme was not necessarily of the order that some advocates of mentoring might expect, nor is it solely or straightforwardly related to the 'mentoring' element of the programme. Thus, in terms of change, it was in relation to social inclusion that the movement was most marked, rather than in relation to offending or drug/alcohol use. In addition, our understanding of how and why individuals change, and of how we can best target particular interventions remains inadequate.

Mentoring Plus rests on a specific model that incorporates a one-to-one mentoring relationship alongside a programme of education and training. The extent to which the success of the programme rested on the mentoring or the Plus element must remain something of an open question, as participants tended to engage actively with both components. Nevertheless, the Plus element appeared to have at least as much impact on the young people as did the mentoring relationship and, on balance, it seems likely that the two main components of the programme tended to reinforce one another. It remains possible that mentoring, in isolation, does not provide an effective way of working with disaffected young people and is best applied as part of a professionally led structured programme. Moreover, as mentoring encountered a greater degree of ambivalence than the Plus component, it may best be used as an *optional* source of support within the context of such programmes.

The impact of Mentoring Plus appeared to be greatest in relation to those areas where the structured activities related directly to the aims of the programme. Thus, seeking to increase young people's involvement in education, training and work was a clearly specified goal both of the programme generally and of the Plus element specifically. By contrast, although reducing offending was a general aim, it was not a specific goal of any of the structured elements of the Plus part of the programme. When set out in these terms, our findings seem unsurprising. And, yet, it is all too often the case that work with young people is undertheorised. That is to say, there is often little explicit discussion of the aims of particular programmes – other than the most banal identification of 'reductions in offending' or something similarly general. The lack of clarity is then compounded by the absence of any explicit model of change. Why is it that a particular intervention might be thought to work? By what means will it change the behaviour of programme participants? In large part, the mentoring programmes in this study rested on a somewhat underspecified model of change. Crucially, although Mentoring Plus had a reasonably well-developed social deficit model, the way in which individuals might achieve change was less well thought through.

The consequence is something of a 'one-size-fits-all' approach to interventions: a programme is designed and established, young people and mentors are recruited and, allowing for a small amount of variation, the model is applied to all those participating. The outcome is that this programme, like all others, appears to have more impact on some young people than others. Now there are many reasons why this might be the case. One possibility, however, is that the method of delivery is appropriate to some, but not all, participants. It is possible that a more developed understanding of individual change would lead – eventually – to a more nuanced model of programme delivery. This, in part, is what we mean by *theory*. Programmes need to develop explicit theories or hypotheses about what they believe 'works' with young people, under what circumstances particular interventions work and, most particularly in this regard, with which young people such interventions are most likely to succeed. This can then be tested and, where appropriate, refined.

Such planning is vital to improvement in the delivery of interventions. This leads us to two final points. First, not only do programmes need a clear model of practice underpinned by an explicit theory of change but, of course, they also need to be implemented as precisely as possible. Clearly, mentoring has benefited in the past from being the latest fashionable idea. The problem, as with all fashions, however, is that things can become unfashionable just as quickly (and irrationally) as they became fashionable. Unless positive outcomes can be demonstrated relatively quickly, there is every likelihood that policy makers and other funders will quickly move on to the next 'silver bullet'.

Under such circumstances, we need not only to try to ensure that interventions operate in an environment of greater security in which the likelihood is that programme integrity is maximised, but also to pay much greater attention to understanding and measuring outcomes. This leads us back to the quote from Sherman and colleagues that we began with at the start of this report. Their plea to government was, rather than ploughing money into yet more unevaluated and unproven programmes, to seek to ensure that there was an increase in carefully controlled evaluations of existing practices. This is something with which we wholeheartedly concur. More particularly, in connection with something like mentoring, there is very clearly a case for the use of experimental research designs. In this study, we adopted as robust a design as was possible under the circumstances at the time – utilising a comparison group and measuring impact over time. Nevertheless, so far as future work in this area is concerned, our view is that random allocation would help to increase our understanding of the relative contributions of mentoring and the Plus element, would begin the process of helping understand the impact of the personal attributes of mentors and mentees in the process of change, and would help to clarify the nature of the links between, for example, increasing involvement in education, training and work, and reductions in offending. Most importantly, it would provide the basis on which we could reorient practice so as to maximise the impact of this particular approach to intervening in the lives of disaffected young people.

73

Notes

Chapter 1

1 For a definition of 'highly engaged' please refer to Chapter 3.

2 The term weighting refers to a process of adjustment whereby more weight is given to cases with certain characteristics than others. In this way, the balance of a sample may be altered to reflect more accurately the population from which it is drawn. Thus, through weighting, we can ensure that respondents to the follow-up surveys reflect the levels of engagement that are evident in the overall sample.

3 As a matter of policy, Mentoring Plus does not match male mentors with female mentees.

4 Crime Concern is an independent national crime reduction charity, which was set up in 1988 with the help of the Home Office. Breaking Barriers was a regeneration initiative run by Crime Concern from 1998 to 2003 in the London boroughs of Camden, Islington and Hackney (http://www.crime.concern.org.uk).

5 The eight London boroughs were: Bexley, Brent, Camden, Hackney, Islington, Lewisham, Lambeth and Newham.

6 The Project Manager was responsible for local fund-raising and day-to-day management of the project. The Education Co-ordinator was primarily responsible for recruiting the young people, implementing a range of social and educational activities, and monitoring contact between the young people and their mentor. The Mentor Co-ordinator was primarily responsible for recruiting, training, supervising and supporting the mentors. The Administrator was primarily responsible for managing the office.

7 Referrals may be considered inappropriate if the young person falls outside the age range on which the projects focus (i.e. 15–19 years old); if the young person has issues which the project feels unable to deal with (e.g. serious mental health issues); or if they are judged to be a threat to other people in the project.

8 In some cases, the mentor and mentee may decide to continue the relationship on an informal basis by meeting less frequently or continuing telephone contact.

Chapter 2

1 In order to facilitate these comparisons, many of the questions in the survey were taken from the *YLS*. Some degree of caution is required, however, as there are notable differences between the surveys. Interviews for the *YLS* were carried out

between October 1998 and January 1999 while the first Mentoring Plus survey was administered from September 2000 to February 2002. While the Mentoring Plus survey took the form of a pen-and-paper survey, the *YLS* was administered via Computer Assisted Personal Interviewing, which has been shown to be particularly well suited to asking questions about sensitive issues (Flood-Page *et al.*, 2000). Unlike the *YLS*, which was administered across the whole of England and Wales and included young people aged 12–30, our survey was limited to the ten areas in which the Mentoring Plus programmes were based and included young people aged 12–19. In order to improve the comparability of the two surveys, data from the *YLS* were weighted to reflect the age and sex profile of the Mentoring Plus cohort. This was achieved by adapting the weights provided with the *YLS*.

2 According to the YLS, 82 per cent of young people aged 17–19 had at least one GCSE and this is less than we might expect given the overall figures for school leavers (95 per cent – see Department for Education and Skills, 2002). This discrepancy reflects the adjustments that were made to the YLS: as the data were weighted to reflect the sex structure of the Mentoring Plus cohort (68 per cent male) and as girls outperform males in their GCSEs, this reduces the estimated proportion of young people with at least one GCSE.

3 The young people were asked if they had ever committed the following offences and, if so, whether or not this had been during the previous 12 months: written or sprayed graffiti on walls, buses, train seats, bus shelters etc; stolen anything worth more than £5; taken a car, motorcycle or moped without the owner's permission, not intending to give it back; driven a car, motorcycle or moped on a public road, without a license and/or insurance; driven a car, motorcycle or moped knowing that you have drunk more than the legal amount of alcohol; stolen anything out of or from a car; damaged or destroyed something – on purpose or recklessly – that belonged to someone else (e.g. a telephone box, car, window of a house); snatched anything from a person – a purse, bag, mobile or anything else; sneaked into a private house, garden or building intending to steal something; bought or sold stolen goods; carried a weapon such as a stick or knife to defend yourself; carried a weapon such as a knife to attack other people; threatened someone with a weapon or threatened to beat them up, in order to get money or other valuables from them; taken part in a fight or disorder in a group or in a public place (e.g. a football ground, riot, or in the street); set fire, on purpose or recklessly, to something (e.g. car, building, garage, dustbins); beaten someone up (belonging to your family, or not) to such an extent that you think medical help was needed; and hurt someone, on purpose, with a stick or other weapon.

4   Graffiti, damaged or destroyed something that belonged to someone else and arson were grouped into a criminal damage category. Stolen something worth more than £5, stolen a car or motorcycle, stolen something out of a car, trespass with intent and bought or sold stolen goods were grouped together as property offences. Snatched something from the person, carrying a weapon to attack other people, threatening someone in order to get money or other valuables from them and taking part in a fight or disorder in a group or in a public place were grouped together as violent offences. Driving without a licence and/or insurance and drunk driving were grouped together as traffic violations.

5   Defined as someone who had committed at least three offences within the last year.

6   Defined as offenders who had ever committed at least one of the following offences: taken a motor vehicle without owner's consent, snatched a purse, etc., trespassed with intent, threats/extortion, assault resulting in medical attention, hurt somebody (on purpose) with a weapon.

7   For these estimates, the *YLS* was weighted to reflect the age and sex profile of the Mentoring Plus cohort. The 95 per cent Confidence Intervals for these estimates were: 4–7 per cent (cautioned), 1–3 per cent (court) and 0–1 per cent (custody).

8   Differences in the questions between our survey and the YLS meant that this comparison was not straightforward. Our survey asked respondents whether they had been drunk while the YLS asked whether they had been *very* drunk. One in four of the young people in the Mentoring Plus cohort indicated that they had been drunk at least once a month during the last year and one in ten indicated that they had been drunk at least once a week during this period (27 per cent and 10 per cent respectively). Within the general population, approximately one in four had been very drunk at least once a month and approximately one in 20 had been very drunk on a weekly basis (20–26 per cent and 3–7 per cent respectively).

9   While black and minority ethnic young people made up a large proportion of the Mentoring Plus cohort, they were much less well represented in the *YLS*.

10 Only three single-substance users had used a drug other than cannabis: two had used cocaine only and one had used solvents only.

11 Current users refer to those who had used an illicit drug (in this case cannabis) during the previous 12 months. The estimate that half of these young people had used cannabis on a daily basis is based on recent research we conducted in two London YOTs. More than four in five (83 per cent) of the young people included in

this study had used cannabis during the previous 12 months and two in three (66 per cent) were using it on a weekly basis. Of those who were using cannabis on a weekly basis, half (51 per cent) were doing so every day (Shiner, unpublished).

12 This term was coined by Ramsay and Percy (1996) to describe stimulants and hallucinogens – amphetamines, LSD, magic mushrooms, ecstasy and amyl nitrate. Recent analysis has shown that, in terms of patterns on use, these substances form a meaningful grouping (Shiner, 2003).

13 This may be a slight exaggeration, as the rate of cocaine use in the general population has increased since 1998/99. According to the British Crime Survey, the proportion of 16–59 year olds who had used cocaine in the last year increased from 1 per cent in 1998 to 2 per cent in 2001/02 (Aust *et al.*, 2002). Even if we double the estimate for the general youthful population based on the 1998/99 *YLS*, however, the resulting figure is still well below that for the Mentoring Plus cohort.

14 All names have been changed to protect identity. While Solomon's was one of the more extreme stories we came across, it highlighted issues that affected many of the young people involved in the programme.

15 The jobs were grouped according to the Standard Occupational Classification 2000. Professional occupations include chemists, doctors, teachers, scientists, probation officers, social workers, accountants, etc. and any other vocation. Associate professionals are those who assist the professionals, e.g. nurses, therapists, IT consultants, youth workers and the like. Personal service occupations are those that involve providing a personal service, e.g. hairdressers, nursery nurses, childminders, etc., and elementary are those people who work as labourers, hospital porters, waitresses and bar staff, postal workers.

Chapter 3

1 The degree of programme integrity achieved by each project was assessed formally through a mixture of quantitative and qualitative measures. Staff turnover was a key measure and was considered to be low if no more than two members of staff left the project during the course of the evaluation, as moderate if three or four members of staff left and as high if five or more members of staff left. The extent to which staff turnover was routine (staff were replaced within three months) or problematic (staff were not replaced within three months) was also taken into account. Qualitative judgements were also made about the extent to

which each project adhered to the Mentoring Plus model and the extent to which the programme was implemented as planned.

2   Project workers were asked to rate how often each of the young people recruited to the programme had engaged with the project and their mentor. Information was provided for 86 per cent of the young people, although some of the projects were unable to provide it: under these circumstances, individuals were classified on the basis of their responses to the first follow-up survey. Using both sources of data, levels of engagement were classified for 93 per cent of the young people recruited to the programme.

3   Active engagement refers to that which took place on a monthly basis or more often.

4   In this context, young people were considered to have engaged actively with the programme if they engaged with the project and/or the mentors on a monthly basis or more often. The rates of engagement given here are based on all of the young people who took part in the recruitment process (those young people who were not recruited to the programme were combined with those who were recruited but did not engage).

5   Although the number of cases was small (only 19 South Asian young people took part in the recruitment process), the difference is sufficiently marked to be considered meaningful.

Chapter 4

1   The analysis presented in this chapter is based on the two follow-up surveys. As the response rate to both these surveys was highest among those young people who engaged most actively with the programme, there was a danger of overstating the possible impact of Mentoring Plus. In order to correct for this possibility, data were weighted so that they reflected the overall level of engagement that was evident within the cohort as a whole.

2   This was assessed through rankings based on the percentage of young people who rated the Plus element and the mentors as 'very helpful'. Four projects were given the same ranking in relation to the mentors and the Plus element; while three projects were ranked one place apart and the remainder were ranked two places apart.

3   Ratings of Mentoring Plus and the mentors (whichever was highest) were used as a proxy measure for the overall helpfulness of the programme.

4   Cramer's V = 0.29 (helpfulness of the programme by project); Kendall's tau-c = 0.13 (helpfulness of the programme by integrity of the programme).

5   Throughout this chapter, figures for the 12 months before the programme are based on individuals who responded to both the initial survey and the first follow-up, as this provides the basis for the most accurate assessment of change over time. It does mean, however, that there may be some discrepancies when compared with figures quoted in previous chapters, as they were based on the entire cohort regardless of whether individuals responded to the follow up survey.

6   By this time, none of the young people in the cohort was permanently excluded from school. Note also that the figure given here for school attendance included those who were truanting regularly. As most of the young people in the cohort had passed the age at which they could legally leave school, questions about truancy were omitted from the second follow-up survey.

7   The young people who were recruited onto the programme but did not engage at all were included in the comparison group.

8   At the start of the programme, 49 per cent of participants were in positions of inclusion and this increased to 63 per cent by the end of the programme: an increase of 14 percentage points, which represented a proportionate increase of 29 per cent (i.e. 14/49 × 100). At the start of the programme, Cramer's V = 0.20 (inclusion/exclusion by participation/non-participation) but, by the end of the programme, Cramer's V = 0.04 (i.e. the difference had all but disappeared).

9   In high-integrity programmes, the percentage of participants in positions of social inclusion increased by 19 points from 46 per cent to 65 per cent, which represented a proportionate increase of 41 per cent (i.e. 19/46 × 100); while, in moderate-integrity programmes, it increased by 18 points, which represented a proportionate increase of 34 per cent (18/53 × 100).

10 Attachment to family was rated as strong if the young person got on well with both parents and as weak if they got on poorly with and/or did not have any contact with both parents. All other situations were rated as moderate attachment.

11 In the 12 months before the programme, 20 per cent of the young people in the cohort carried a weapon to attack somebody and this fell to 8 per cent in the following 12 months: a decrease of 12 percentage points, which represents a proportionate decrease of 60 per cent (i.e. 12/20 × 100).

12 Some care is required here, as the figures relate to different time frames. In the initial survey and the first follow-up, questions were asked about a 12-month period, while, in the second survey, questions were asked about a six-month period.

13 Among participants in projects with a high degree of integrity, the proportion of persistent offenders fell from 66 per cent in the 12 months prior to the programme to 42 per cent during the 12 months covered by the programme and to 22 per cent during the six months after the end of the programme. A very similar profile was evident among participants in projects with a low degree of integrity: within this group, the rate of persistent offending fell from 62 to 41 per cent and to 22 per cent. A less marked fall was evident among participants in projects with a moderate degree of integrity (40 per cent to 33 per cent to 20 per cent).

14 Among those who moved from a position of exclusion to inclusion between the start and end of the programme, the proportion of persistent offenders fell from 65 per cent in the 12 months prior to the programme to 51 per cent during the 12 months covered by the programme and to 28 per cent during the six months after the end of the programme. Among those who were in a position of social exclusion at the beginning and end of the programme, the rate of persistent offending fell from 77 to 27 per cent and to 22 per cent.

15 Among those who indicated that the programme had helped to tackle their offending behaviour, the proportion of persistent offenders fell by 72 per cent (68–19/68 × 100). Among those who did not indicate that the programme had helped them in this way, the proportion of persistent offenders fell by 64 per cent (53–19/53 × 100).

16 Participants were more likely to smoke than non-participants and this difference became slightly more marked during the period covered by the programme. The proportion of participants who were daily smokers increased (from 45 to 56 per cent) while the proportion of non-participants who were daily smokers fell (from 39 to 35 per cent). The proportion of non-smokers in each group remained fairly consistent (40 per cent and 36 per cent for participants and 54 per cent and 56 per cent for non-participants). At the start and end of the programme, Cramer's V = 0.16 and 0.21 respectively (smoking by participation in the programme).

17 At the start and end of the programme, Cramer's V = 0.14 and 0.08 respectively (drinking by participation) and 0.14 and 0.12 respectively (drunkenness by participation).

18 This overall pattern of consistency carried over into the six months after the programme. Of those who used drugs during the 12 months prior to the programme, 83 per cent continued to do so in the six months after the programme and 76 per cent of those who had not done so continued not to. Cramer's V = 0.48 (used drugs in 12 months prior to the programme by used drugs in the 12 months covered by the programme) and 0.59 (used drugs in 12 months prior to the programme by used drugs in the six months after the programme).

19 The proportion of participants who used each of the substances (or group of substances) shown in Figure 14 during the year of the programme was within one or two percentage points of the proportion who had done so during the 12 months prior to the programme. Similarly, the proportion of non-participants who used each of these substances during the year of the programme was within three percentage points of the proportion who had done so during the 12 months previously. Finally, the differences between the proportion of participants and non-participants who used these substances during these two periods changed by no more than three percentage points. Thus, for example, while 60 per cent of participants and 46 per cent of non-participants used cannabis in the year before the programme (a difference of 14 per cent), 62 per cent and 47 per cent did so respectively in the following year (a difference of 15 per cent).

20 Self-esteem at the start of the programme was classified according to the percentile values so that four groups of approximately equal size were produced. The categories do not have any external validity outside of the cohort and simply indicate how individuals' scores compared with those of other members of the cohort.

References

Audit Commission (1996) *Misspent Youth: Young People and Crime*. London: Audit Commission

Aust, R., Sharp, C. and Goulden, C. (2002) *Prevalence of Drug Use: Key Findings from the 2001/2002 British Crime Survey*. London: Home Office

Bandura, A. (1977) *Social Learning Theory*. Englewood Cliffs, NJ: Prentice-Hall

Benioff, S. (1997) *A Second Chance: Developing Mentoring and Education Projects for Young People*. London: Dalston Youth Project/Crime Concern

Bowling, B. and Phillips, C. (2002) *Racism, Crime and Justice*. Harlow: Longman

Cabinet Office (2000) *Minority Ethnic Issues and Social Exclusion and Neighbourhood Renewal: A Guide to the Work of the Social Exclusion Unit and the Policy Action Teams so Far*. London: Cabinet Office

Crime Concern (undated[a]) *Mentoring Plus*. London: Crime Concern

Crime Concern (undated[b]) *Mentoring Work with Minority Ethnic Young People*. London: Crime Concern

Department for Education and Skills (2002) *National Statistics: First Release – GCSE/GNVQ Results for Young People in England, 2001/02 (Early Statistics)*. London: Department for Education and Skills

Flood-Page, C., Campbell, S., Harrington, V. and Miller, J. (2000) *Youth Crime: Findings from the 1998/99 Youth Lifestyles Survey*. London: Home Office

Hollin, C.R. (1995) 'The meaning and implications of programme integrity', in J. McGuire (ed.) *What Works: Reducing Reoffending*. Chichester: Wiley

McGuire, J. (1995) *What Works: Reducing Reoffending*. Chichester: Wiley

Mair, G., Lloyd, C., Nee, C. and Sibbitt, R. (1994) *Intensive Probation in England and Wales: An Evaluation*. London: Home Office

Modood, T., Berthoud, R., Lakey, J., Nazroo, J., Smith, P., Virdee, S. and Beishon, A. (1997) *Diversity and Disadvantage: Ethnic Minorities in Britain*. London: Policy Studies Institute

Newburn, T. (1993) *Disaster and After: Social Work in the Aftermath of Disaster*. London: Jessica Kingsley

Newburn, T. and Shiner, M. (2001) *Teenage Kicks? Young People and Alcohol: A Review of the Literature*. York: Joseph Rowntree Foundation

Parker, H., and Bottomley, T. (1996) *Crack Cocaine and Drugs – Crime Careers*. London: Home Office

Ramsay, M., and Percy, A. (1996) *Drug Misuse Declared: Results of the 1994 British Crime Survey.* London: Home Office

Robinson, J.P., Shaver, P.R. and Wrightsman, L.S. (1991) *Measures of Personality and Social Psychological Attitudes.* London: Academic Press

Rosenberg, M. (1965) *Society and the Adolescent Self-image.* Princeton, NJ: University Press.

Sangster, D., Shiner, M., Patel, K. and Sheikh, N. (2002) *Delivery of Drug Services to Black and Minority Ethnic Communities.* London: Home Office

Sherman, L.W., Gottfredson, D., MacKenzie, D., Eck, J., Reuter, P. and Bushway, S. (1997) *Preventing Crime: What Works, What Doesn't, What's Promising.* Maryland: Department of Criminology and Criminal Justice, University of Maryland. http://www.ncjrs.org/works

Sheroff, M.R. (1983) 'Fifty volunteers', in S. Hatch (ed.) *Volunteers: Patterns, Meanings and Motives.* Berkhamsted: The Volunteer Centre

Shiner, M. (unpublished) 'Merton and Sutton YAP/YOT prevention, early intervention, treatment and support project', available from author, m.shiner@lse.ac.uk

Shiner, M. (2003) 'Out of harm's way? Illicit drug use, medicalization and the law', *British Journal of Criminology*, Vol. 43, No. 4, pp. 772–96

Smith, D. and McVie, S. (2003) 'Theory and method in the Edinburgh study of youth transitions and crime', *British Journal of Criminology*, Vol. 43, No. 1, pp. 169–95

Stratford, N., and Roth, W. (1999) *The 1998 Youth Lifestyles Survey: Technical Report.* London: National Centre for Social Research

Appendix 1
Tables

Table A1.1 Current status, orientation to school and qualifications (per cent)

	Mentoring Plus cohort	General youthful population Estimate	General youthful population Range
Current status			
Attending school	46	74	71–77
Studying at college/university	8	13	11–15
On a training scheme	5	2	1–3
Working	1	7	6–9
Disengaged	40	4	3–5
Truanting from school			
Every week	34	5	4–7
Two or three days a month	18	1	1–2
Less often	17	14	12–16
Not at all	31	79	77–82
Attitudes to school			
Like it a lot	16	35	32–38
Like it a little	22	35	32–37
Neither/nor	21	14	11–16
Dislike it a little	11	7	6–9
Dislike it a lot	30	9	7–11
Qualifications (17–19 year olds only)			
GCSE	47	82	77–86
NVQ Foundation/Intermediate	17	3	1–4
BTEC Certificate	2	4	1–6
City and Guilds	13	6	3–8

Source: Mentoring Plus cohort (first survey) and YLS (1998/99).
Note: the 1998/99 YLS was adjusted to reflect the age and sex structure of the Mentoring Plus cohort.

Table A1.2 Comparative rates of offending (per cent)

	Mentoring Plus cohort	General youthful population Estimate	General youthful population Range
Committed an offence			
No, never	7	42	39–45
Yes – but not in last 12 months	8	20	17–23
Yes – in last 12 months	85	38	35–41
Criminal damage			
No, never	31	67	64–70
Yes – but not in last 12 months	16	18	15–21
Yes – in last 12 months	54	15	13–18
Property offences			
No, never	27	71	68–74
Yes – but not in last 12 months	14	13	11–15
Yes – in last 12 months	60	16	14–19

(Continued)

Table A1.2 Comparative rates of offending (per cent) (continued)

	Mentoring Plus cohort	General youthful population Estimate	General youthful population Range
Violent offences			
No, never	22	76	73–78
Yes – but not in last 12 months	14	10	8–12
Yes – in last 12 months	64	14	12–17
Traffic violations			
No, never	50	78	75–81
Yes – but not in last 12 months	8	10	7–12
Yes – in last 12 months	42	13	10–15
Persistent offender			
No	38	89	87–91
Yes	62	11	9–13
Serious offence			
No, never	30	85	82–87
Yes – but not in last 12 months	13	7	5–9
Yes – in last 12 months	57	8	6–10

Source: Mentoring Plus cohort (first survey) and YLS (1998/99).

Note: the 1998/99 YLS was adjusted to reflect the age and sex structure of the Mentoring Plus cohort.

Table A1.3 Comparative rates of illicit drug use (per cent)

	Mentoring Plus cohort	General youthful population Estimate	General youthful population Range
Cannabis			
Used in the last 12 months	60	24	21–27
Used but not in last 12 months	10	6	4–7
Never used	30	70	67–73
Hallucinants			
Used in the last 12 months	10	9	7–10
Used but not in last 12 months	5	5	4–7
Never used	85	86	84–89
Solvents			
Used in the last 12 months	4	4	3–5
Used but not in last 12 months	3	4	3–6
Never used	93	92	90–94
Cocaine			
Used in the last 12 months	7	1	0–2
Used but not in last 12 months	3	1	0–2
Never used	90	98	97–99
Crack and/or heroin			
Used in the last 12 months	4	0.3	0–1
Used but not in last 12 months	3	0.5	0–1
Never used	94	99	98–100

Source: Mentoring Plus cohort (first survey) and YLS (1998/99).

Note: the 1998/99 YLS was adjusted to reflect the age and sex structure of the Mentoring Plus cohort.

Appendix 2
Rosenberg's measure of self-esteem

Rosenberg (1965) viewed self-esteem as an evaluative *attitude*, that is, a generally positive or negative feeling about oneself. High self-esteem would mean that the individual respects him or herself for what he/she is, considers him or herself worthy (but does not necessarily consider him or herself better than others); while low self-esteem was seen to imply 'self-rejection, self-dissatisfaction, self-contempt' (Rosenberg, 1965, p. 31). Rosenberg's scale was one of the first attempts to measure self-esteem and continues to be widely used. It has a low level of error and is known to produce very similar results on successive occasions; it was originally devised to study adolescents and seemed appropriate for our study; and is fairly short and was thus considered to be well suited to our purpose, given that we also wanted to focus on many other questions.

Rosenberg's scale is based on the following statements:

1   On the whole, I am satisfied with myself.

2   At times I think I am no good at all.

3   I feel that I have a number of good qualities.

4   I am able to do things as well as most other people.

5   I feel I do not have much to be proud of.

6   I certainly feel useless at times.

7   I feel that I'm a person of worth, at least on an equal plane with others.

8   I wish I could have more respect for myself.

9   All in all, I am inclined to feel that I am a failure.

10 I take a positive attitude toward myself.

Responses to these statements were sought using a four-point scale of agreement, from strongly agree to strongly disagree. For negatively worded items (i.e. 2, 5, 6, 8 and 9), the scoring system was reversed and responses were converted into scores ranging from 10 to 40, where low scores indicated high self-esteem and high scores indicated low self-esteem. Although the scale is widely used, there are no established norms regarding which scores and/or cut-off points can be seen as reflecting high or low self-esteem.